THE
VIEWPOINTS
BOOK

THE VIEWPOINTS BOOK

A Practical Guide
to Viewpoints
and Composition

ANNE BOGART

AND

TINA LANDAU

THEATRE COMMUNICATIONS GROUP
NEW YORK
2005

This publication is made possible in part with funds from the New York State
Council on the Arts, a State Agency.

TCG books are exclusively distributed to the book trade by Consortium Book Sales
and Distribution.

LIBRARY OF CONGRESS CATALOGING-IN-PUBLICATION DATA

Bogart, Anne
The viewpoints book : a practical guide to viewpoints and composition / By Anne
Bogart and Tina Landau.—1st ed.
p. cm.
ISBN-13: 978-1-55936-241-2
ISBN-10: 1-55936-241-3 (pbk. : alk. paper)
1. Movement (Acting) 2. Improvisation (Acting) I. Landau, Tina. II. Title.
PN2071.M6B64 2004
792.02'8—dc22
2004024021

Cover design by Mark Melnick
Cover image by Megan Wanlass Szalla
Cover calligraphy by Doctor Bennett
Author photos by Dixie Sheridan (Bogart) and Michal Daniel (Landau)
Book design and composition by Lisa Govan

First Edition, November 2005
Seventh Printing, September 2012

For the performers
whose bodies and imaginations
carry this work forward

CONTENTS

PREFACE

"What can I read on Viewpoints?"

The question has been asked of us with increasing regularity over recent years. When either one of us comes close to concluding a class, workshop or production, the questioning often begins: "How do I continue the work?" "How do I apply this to scene work?" "How can I use this in writing my play?" "What if I'm working with people who have not done Viewpoints training?" "What other exercises are there in Composition work?" This book was born out of a desire to answer *some* of the questions we have been asked over the years.

There is not a lot of available material on Viewpoints. There are some articles and essays but, as far as we know, there is no book devoted to the subject, let alone what we have hoped to write here: a comprehensive nuts-and-bolts approach to the uses of Viewpoints. This is not a book on theory, but a practical how-to guide through the stages and applications of the work.

We wrote this book so that our students, actors, collaborators and even skeptics could have something to refer to when desired.

The Viewpoints Book is not definitive, not gospel, not absolute truth. It is written out of personal experience and belief. While we both stand firmly by the notion that Viewpoints is an open process rather than a closed methodology, we do hope that anyone interested in the work will approach it with depth and rigor and the same soul-searching that we both hope *we* have done over the years. Our wish is not that these pages be read as a prescriptive instruction manual, but rather as an array of possibilities, a call to further examination and personalization on the part of the reader.

There *are* steps and basics that we believe are crucial for understanding Viewpoints in the body, and for using it most effectively in training and rehearsal. We have outlined these. There are lazy or undigested ways of teaching Viewpoints and, even more so, talking about it, and people are doing this more and more frequently. But our solution is not that one reads these pages and follows them as dictated. We'd all love an answer, a guarantee, a shortcut. Viewpoints training provides none of these. Although we are laying the work out in a very linear and structured fashion, it's deadly for any artist to mechanically try to follow the steps without wrestling with the questions, adjusting the process, and earning their own discoveries. We hope you read these pages and question. We hope you read them and try. We hope you use them, then write on them, then *re*write them, then read them again.

We wrote this book by splitting up the outline, each taking first passes at the chapters we felt strongest about. Then we traded material, adding to each other's work, cutting each other's work, revising together. We made a choice to write from the "we" because the book reflects those things we share as beliefs and practices. Occasionally, in wanting to offer a specific example, we refer to our own productions or experiences: "When Anne directed . . ." or "When Tina directed . . ."

We had difficulty in determining the appropriate syntax in writing to *you*. Are *you* the instructor, the director, a performer, designer, playwright? Leader or participant? For the most part, we have addressed this book to the person leading the work—the teacher or director. But you will notice that we sometimes fluidly, and perhaps inconsistently, float into becoming the teacher's or director's voice ourselves. We might begin an exercise with: "First you gather the group in the center of the space and have everyone close her/his eyes . . ." (addressing the leader), but soon transition into: "Sense the bodies around you, and listen to the sound of breathing . . ." (addressing the participants).

We are also aware that, due to the nature of the subject and the fact that we wrote in tandem, there are many times throughout the book when a topic is revisited, addressed a second or even a third time. We hope we have repeated ourselves within a new context or with a slightly altered perspective.

Each of us was introduced to Viewpoints by another person: Anne from Mary Overlie at New York University, Tina from Anne at the American Repertory Theatre. Both of us went through our own process: first, feeling that the world had been named, that we now had words for what we had always intuited or done; second, becoming seduced by the system itself, its power, its effect, its style; and third, recognizing the need for reexamination and reshaping of the technique to reflect our own passions and observations. In writing down many of the exercises in this book, we found ourselves remembering in vivid detail the moments in which we first created them. Almost always, the exercises were born out of moments of terror: "I have six hours and twenty actors and what am I going to do?!"

We are torn between the desire to provide a map for you and the desire to tell you to rip up this book and enter the terror for yourself. As Joseph Campbell has said: "Where you stumble, there you shall find your treasure." We invite the stumbling. We hope maybe to have indicated a path but not cleared it, leaving you to work through the most thorny areas. Viewpoints is an open process, not a rigid technique. We hope that this book will be for you not an end but a beginning.

Anne Bogart and Tina Landau
October 2005

We would like to acknowledge the following people for their contributions to this book and to our lives:

Mary Overlie, who forged the original Six Viewpoints from her imagination. Aileen Passloff, who extended the notion of Composition from the dance world into the arena of theater. Wendell Beavers, who carries Viewpoints with him everywhere. The individual members of SITI Company, who have developed and expanded the Viewpoints over years of practice, rehearsal and teaching, in particular Barney O'Hanlon, who is a constant innovator, experimenter and inspiration. Charles L. Mee, Jr., Brian Jucha, Ron Argelander, Susan Milani, Kevin Kuhlke, Jessica Litwak, John Bernd, Mark Russell, Jocelyn Clarke, Sabine Andreas,

—A. B.

Theresa McCarthy, Henry Stram, Martin Moran, Jessica Molaskey, Victoria Clark, Jason Daniely, Steven Skybell, Jeff Perry, Amy Morton and Guy Adkins, among others—my Viewpoint muses, who have taught me everything I know about how to apply and integrate the work in rehearsal. Anne Hamburger, Marjorie Samoff, Robert Brustein, Richard Riddell, Michael David, Martha Lavey, the memory of Helen Merrill, and SITI company—all of whom supported me so generously along the way.

—T. L.

And, of course, from both of us: Terry Nemeth and Kathy Sova, for their clarity in helping us find a shape for this book.

THE
VIEWPOINTS
BOOK

CHAPTER I

A HISTORY OF VIEWPOINTS AND COMPOSITION

A seismic cultural shift occurred in America during the middle of the last century. It was a shift marked by such events as the protests against the Vietnam War, the marches for civil rights, and the birth of abstract expressionism, postmodernism and minimalism. During the 1960s, this cultural explosion and artistic revolution gained momentum in New York City, San Francisco and other urban centers and then spread across the nation. The movement was political, aesthetic and personal, and it altered the way artists thought about their processes, their audiences and their role in the world. This sudden eruption of activity was like a breath of fresh air for many young people, including a group of artists—the Judson Church Theater—who united together at the Judson Church on Washington Square in New York City. The group included the young painters Robert Rauschenberg and Jasper Johns, composers John Cage and Philip Corner, filmmaker Gene Friedman, and dancers Yvonne Rainer, Trisha Brown, David Gordon, Lucinda Childs, Steve Paxton, Laura

Dean, Simone Forti and others. Inspired by their dance composition teacher, Robert Dunn, these dancers wanted to question the assumptions of their own training and how they approached their work. They wanted to create alternatives to the pervasive influence of George Balanchine, Martha Graham and even closer contemporaries, like Merce Cunningham. They wanted to liberate choreography from psychology and conventional drama. "What is dance?" they asked. "If an elephant swings its trunk, is it dance? If a person walks across the stage, is that dance?"

A number of experiments ensued: performances on rooftops, audiences witnessing events through keyholes, dancers suspended in midair, dancers on rolling platforms. Working with the notion that anything is possible, these artists started to change the rules. Rauschenberg and Johns, for example, not only created designs for the performances but often conceived the events and performed in them. Improvisation became the common language and everyone helped each other out.

One of the fundamental agreements that united this group was their belief in nonhierarchical art and the use of "real time" activities which were arrived at through game-like structures or task-oriented activities. The group wanted to function democratically with all members having equal access to performance opportunities. In improvisations, each participant had the same power in the creation of an event. The aesthetic thinking was also nonhierarchical. Music, for example, would not dictate choices. An object could have the same importance as a human body. The spoken word could be on equal footing with gesture. One idea could hold the same importance as another on the same stage at the same time.

These postmodern pioneers forged the territory upon which we now stand. They rejected the insistence by the modern dance world upon social messages and virtuosic technique, and replaced it with internal decisions, structures, rules or problems. What made the final dance was the context of the dance. Whatever movement occurred while working on these problems *became* the art. This philosophy lies at the heart of both Viewpoints and Composition.

In the early 1970s, Aileen Passloff, a dancer and choreographer and an influential touchstone in the Judson Church Movement, became Anne's professor at Bard College. Aileen's composition class had an enormous effect on the way Anne began to think about creating work. The students were asked to create their own work based on dreams, objects, advertisements, whatever might seem fodder for creation. For Anne, this was the genesis of a lifetime's interest in applying theories of painting, architecture, music and film to theater. Aileen also inspired Anne to investigate the creative role of each performer.

Later, in 1979, Anne met choreographer Mary Overlie, the inventor of the "Six Viewpoints," at New York University, where they were both on the faculty of the Experimental Theater Wing. Although a latecomer to the Judson scene, Mary, who had trained as a dancer and choreographer, attributes her own innovations to those Judson Church experiments. Her thinking was also ignited by colleagues in San Francisco, including Anna Halprin in Berkeley, Deborah Hay and, particularly, Barbara Dilley, who, with Mary, brought together an all-women's group called the Natural History of the American Dancer.

Mary immersed herself in these innovations and came up with her own way to structure dance improvisation in time and space—the Six Viewpoints: Space, Shape, Time, Emotion, Movement and Story. She began to apply these principles, not only to her own work as choreographer, but also to her teaching. Subsequently, her work has influenced several generations of theater artists.

Mary's approach to the Six Viewpoints was and continues to be absolute. She is adamant about their purity. To her chagrin and delight, her students and colleagues, recognizing the genius of her innovations and their immediate relevance to the theater, have extrapolated and expanded her Viewpoints for their own uses.

To Anne (and later Tina), it was instantly clear that Mary's approach to generating movement for the stage was applicable to creating viscerally dynamic moments of theater with actors and other collaborators. In 1987, Tina and Anne met while working at the American Repertory Theatre in Cambridge, MA. Over the next ten years, they collaborated extensively, experimented theatrically, and gradually expanded Overlie's Six Viewpoints to both nine Physical Viewpoints (Spatial Relationship, Kinesthetic Response, Shape, Gesture, Repetition, Architecture, Tempo, Duration and Topography) and Vocal Viewpoints (Pitch, Dynamic, Acceleration/Deceleration, Silence and Timbre).

Over the past twenty years, Viewpoints training has ignited the imaginations of choreographers, actors, directors, designers, dramaturgs and writers. While the Viewpoints are now taught all over the world and used by many theater artists in the rehearsal process, the theory and its application are still relatively new. The questions arise frequently: What exactly *is* Viewpoints? What exactly *is* Composition?

CHAPTER 2

VIEWPOINTS AND COMPOSITION: WHAT ARE THEY?

Viewpoints, Composition: What do these terms mean? The following definitions reflect *our* understanding and use of them. Even in the context of the work of such pioneers as Mary Overlie and Aileen Passloff, it is impossible to say where these ideas actually originated, because they are timeless and belong to the natural principles of movement, time and space. Over the years, we have simply articulated a set of names for things that already exist, things that we do naturally and have always done, with greater or lesser degrees of consciousness and emphasis.

VIEWPOINTS

□ Viewpoints is a philosophy translated into a technique for (1) training performers; (2) building ensemble; and (3) creating movement for the stage.

- Viewpoints is a set of names given to certain principles of movement through time and space; these names constitute a language for talking about what happens onstage.
- Viewpoints is points of awareness that a performer or creator makes use of while working.

We work with nine Physical Viewpoints, within Viewpoints of Time and Viewpoints of Space. The bulk of this book focuses on the Physical Viewpoints, though Vocal Viewpoints, which we developed later, are addressed in Chapter 9. The Vocal Viewpoints are specifically related to sound as opposed to movement. Physical and Vocal Viewpoints overlap each other and constantly change in relative value, depending on the artist or teacher and/or the style of the production. The Physical Viewpoints are:

Viewpoints of Time

TEMPO

The rate of speed at which a movement occurs; how fast or slow something happens onstage.

DURATION

How long a movement or sequence of movements continues. Duration, in terms of Viewpoints work, specifically relates to how long a group of people working together stay inside a certain section of movement before it changes.

KINESTHETIC RESPONSE

A spontaneous reaction to motion which occurs outside you; the timing in which you respond to the external events of movement or sound; the impulsive movement that occurs from a stimulation of the senses. An example: someone claps in front of your eyes and you blink in response; or someone slams a door and you impulsively stand up from your chair.

REPETITION

The repeating of something onstage. Repetition includes (1) *Internal Repetition* (repeating a movement within your own body); (2) *External Repetition* (repeating the shape, tempo, gesture, etc., of something outside your own body).

Viewpoints of Space

SHAPE

The contour or outline the body (or bodies) makes in space. All Shape can be broken down into either (1) *lines*; (2) *curves*; (3) a *combination* of lines and curves.

Therefore, in Viewpoints training we create shapes that are round, shapes that are angular, shapes that are a mixture of these two.

In addition, Shape can either be (1) *stationary*; (2) *moving* through space.

Lastly, Shape can be made in one of three forms: (1) the body in space; (2) the body in relationship to architecture making a shape; (3) the body in relationship to other bodies making a shape.

GESTURE

A movement involving a part or parts of the body; Gesture is Shape with a beginning, middle and end. Gestures can be made with the hands, the arms, the legs, the head, the mouth, the eyes, the feet, the stomach, or any other part or combination of parts that can be isolated. Gesture is broken down into:

1. BEHAVIORAL GESTURE. Belongs to the concrete, physical world of human behavior as we observe it in our everyday reality. It is the kind of gesture you see in the supermarket or on the subway: scratching, pointing, waving, sniffing, bowing, saluting. A Behavioral Gesture can give informa-

tion about character, time period, physical health, circumstance, weather, clothes, etc. It is usually defined by a person's character or the time and place in which they live. It can also have a thought or intention behind it. A Behavioral Gesture can be further broken down and worked on in terms of *Private Gesture* and *Public Gesture*, distinguishing between actions performed in solitude and those performed with awareness of or proximity to others.

2. EXPRESSIVE GESTURE. Expresses an inner state, an emotion, a desire, an idea or a value. It is abstract and symbolic rather than representational. It is universal and timeless and is not something you would normally see someone do in the supermarket or subway. For instance, an Expressive Gesture might be expressive of, or stand for, such emotions as "joy," "grief" or "anger." Or it might express the inner essence of Hamlet as a given actor feels him. Or, in a production of Chekhov, you might create and work with Expressive Gestures *of* or *for* "time," "memory" or "Moscow."

ARCHITECTURE

The physical environment in which you are working and how awareness of it affects movement. How many times have we seen productions where there is a lavish, intricate set covering the stage and yet the actors remain down center, hardly exploring or using the surrounding architecture? In working on Architecture as a Viewpoint, we learn to dance with the space, to be in dialogue with a room, to let movement (especially Shape and Gesture) evolve out of our surroundings. Architecture is broken down into:

1. SOLID MASS. Walls, floors, ceilings, furniture, windows, doors, etc.
2. TEXTURE. Whether the solid mass is wood or metal or fabric will change the kind of movement we create in relationship to it.
3. LIGHT. The sources of light in the room, the shadows we make in relationship to these sources, etc.

4. COLOR. Creating movement off of colors in the space, e.g., how one red chair among many black ones would affect our choreography in relation to that chair.
5. SOUND. Sound created by and from the architecture, e.g., the sound of feet on the floor, the creak of a door, etc.

Additionally, in working with Architecture, we create *spatial metaphors*, giving form to such feelings as I'm "up against the wall," "caught between the cracks," "trapped," "lost in space," "on the threshold," "high as a kite," etc.

SPATIAL RELATIONSHIP

The distance between things onstage, especially (1) one body to another; (2) one body (or bodies) to a group of bodies; (3) the body to the architecture.

What is the full range of possible distances between things onstage? What kinds of groupings allow us to see a stage picture more clearly? Which groupings suggest an event or emotion, express a dynamic? In both real life and onstage, we tend to position ourselves at a polite two- or three-foot distance from someone we are talking to. When we become aware of the expressive possibilities of Spatial Relationship onstage, we begin working with less polite but more dynamic distances of extreme proximity or extreme separation.

TOPOGRAPHY

The *landscape*, the *floor pattern*, the *design* we create in movement through space. In defining a landscape, for instance, we might decide that the downstage area has great density, is difficult to move through, while the upstage area has less density and therefore involves more fluidity and faster tempos. To understand floor pattern, imagine that the bottoms of your feet are painted red; as you move through the space, the picture that evolves on the floor is the floor pattern that emerges over time. In addition, staging or designing for performance always involves choices about the *size* and *shape* of the space we work in. For example, we might choose to work in a narrow three-foot strip all the way downstage or in a giant triangular shape that covers the whole floor, etc.

COMPOSITION

- Composition is a method for creating new work.
- Composition is the practice of selecting and arranging the separate components of theatrical language into a cohesive work of art for the stage. It is the same technique that any choreographer, painter, writer, composer or filmmaker uses in their corresponding disciplines. In theater, it is *writing on your feet*, with others, in space and time, using the language of theater.
- Composition is a method for generating, defining and developing the theater vocabulary that will be used for any given piece. In Composition, we make pieces so that we can point to them and say: "That worked," and ask: "Why?" so that we can then articulate which ideas, moments, images, etc., we will include in our production.
- Composition is a method for revealing to ourselves our hidden thoughts and feelings about the material. Because we usually make Compositions in rehearsal in a compressed period of time, we have no time to think. Composition provides a structure for working from our impulses and intuition. As Pablo Picasso once said, making art is "another way of keeping a diary."
- Composition is an assignment given to an ensemble so that it can create short, specific theater pieces addressing a particular aspect of the work. We use Composition during rehearsal to engage the collaborators in the process of generating their own work around a source. The assignment will usually include an overall intention or structure as well as a substantial list of ingredients which must be included in the piece. This list is the raw material of the theater lan-

guage we'll speak in the piece, either principles that are use-ful for staging (symmetry versus asymmetry, use of scale and perspective, juxtaposition, etc.) or the ingredients that belong specifically to the Play-World we are working on (objects, textures, colors, sounds, actions, etc.) These ingre-dients are to a Composition what single words are to a para-graph or essay. The creator makes meaning through their arrangement.

- Composition is a method for being in dialogue with other art forms, as it borrows from and reflects the other arts. In Composition work, we study and use principles from other disciplines translated for the stage. For example, borrowing from music, we might ask what the rhythm of a moment is, or how to interact based on a fugue structure, or how a coda functions and whether or not we should add one. Or we'll think about film: "How do we stage a close-up? An estab-lishing shot? A montage?" And we'll ask: "What is the equivalent in the theater?" In applying Compositional principles from other disciplines to the theater, we push the envelope of theatrical possibility and challenge ourselves to create new forms.
- Composition is to the creator (whether director, writer, per-former, designer, etc.) what Viewpoints is to the actor: a method for practicing the art.

CHAPTER 3

VIEWPOINTS AND COMPOSITION IN CONTEMPORARY THEATER

Viewpoints and Composition offer an alternative to conventional approaches to acting, directing, playwriting and design. They represent a clear-cut procedure and attitude that is nonhierarchical, practical and collaborative in nature. Both address particular problems and assumptions that a young person faces when entering the field, and offer an alternative.

Young theater artists inherit the following formidable problems as they enter into the American theater arena:

Problem 1: The Americanization of the Stanislavsky system.

The approach to acting for the stage in the United States has not changed much over the past sixty or seventy years. Our misunderstanding, misappropriation and miniaturization of the Stanislavsky system remains the bible for most practitioners. Like the air we breathe, we are rarely aware of its dominance and omnipresence.

In 1923, Konstantin Stanislavsky and his company, the Moscow Art Theatre, arrived in the United States to perform a repertory of plays by Gorky and Chekhov. The approach to acting on display in those productions had a galvanizing impact on young theater artists. Inspired by the performances, and curious to learn more, Americans grasped onto what turned out to be a severely limited aspect of Stanislavsky's "system," and turned it into a religion. Highly effective for film and television, this legacy has meanwhile shackled the American theater to an ultrarealistic approach to the art of the stage. Later, Stanislavsky admitted that his earlier psychological methods, which had been so influential in the United States, were misguided. He then altered his emphasis from inducing emotion through affective memory to a system of psycho-physical chain-of-action, where *action*, rather than psychology, induced emotion and feeling.

The inherited problems and assumptions caused by the Americanization of the Stanislavsky system are unmistakably evident in rehearsal when you hear an actor say: "If I feel it, the audience will feel it," or "I'll do it when I feel it." When a rehearsal boils down to the process of manufacturing and then hanging desperately onto emotion, genuine human interaction is sacrificed. Emotion induced by recollection of past experience can quickly turn acting into a solipsistic exercise. The Herculean effort to pin down a particular emotion removes the actor from the simple task of performing an action, and thereby distances actors from one another and from the audience. Instead of forcing and fixing an emotion, Viewpoints training allows untamed feeling to arise from the actual physical, verbal and imaginative situation in which actors find themselves together.

Another misconception about Stanislavky's theories of acting supposes that all onstage action is motivated exclusively by psychological intention. Therefore, we are often faced with actors who need to know: "What is my objective?" or "What do I want?"

before they are willing to make a move. Often this resistance is followed by the statement: "My character would never do that."

Viewpoints and Composition suggest fresh ways of making choices onstage and generating action based on awareness of time and space in addition to or instead of psychology.

Problem 2: Lack of ongoing actor training.

The theater is the only artistic discipline that does not encourage or insist upon the ongoing training of its practitioners. The result: rusty or inflexible actors who often feel unsatisfied or uninspired.

What musician, after graduating from a conservatory, would assume that s/he did not need to practice every day? What dancer would not take class or do bar exercises on a regular basis? What painter, what singer, what writer would not practice her/his art daily? And yet, upon graduation from a training program, actors are supposed to be ready for the marketplace without a commitment to ongoing personal training.

Training forges relationships, develops skill and provides an opportunity for continued growth. Viewpoints training and Composition work allow actors and their collaborators to practice creating fiction together on a daily basis using the tools of time and space. This daily practice keeps the artistic juices flowing, creates cohesive ensembles and allows individuals and groups to practice speaking the language of the stage.

Problem 3: The word "want" and its effect upon rehearsal atmosphere and production.

The word "want" is generally used too often and too carelessly in our working environment. Is it correct to assume that the actor's job is to do what the director "wants," and the director's job to know above all else what s/he wants and demand it?

The specific language used during a rehearsal impacts the quality of relationships between people as well as the tone of the environment. The word *"want"*—much overused and abused in our American system of rehearsing a play—implies a right and wrong. It encourages artists to search for a single satisfying choice, driven by seeking approval from an absolute authority above them.

Many young directors assume that their job is to know what they *want* and to insist on it by saying things like: "Now I *want* you to cross the stage and pick up the teacup." Actors assume too often that their job, first and foremost, is to do what the director *wants*. How often can an actor ask a director: "Is this what you *want*?" before the contribution of that actor is completely negated? Why not ask instead what the *play* wants? The director and the actor are then united in a mutual endeavor. The word *"want,"* used habitually and without consciousness of the consequences, constructs a parent/child relationship in rehearsal. This parent/child relationship limits resiliency, rigor and maturity in the creative process and inhibits true collaboration.

Can the artistic process be collaborative? Can a group of strong-minded individuals *together* ask what the play or project *wants*, rather than depending upon the hierarchical domination of one person? Of course a project needs structure and a sense of direction but can the leader aim for discovery rather than staging a replica of what s/he has decided beforehand? Can we resist proclaiming "what it is" long enough to authentically ask: "What is it?"

The exploration of a theme, the discovery of staging and the excavation of language, for instance, can all be a collective act in which ideas are proposed and adjustments made by all parties. Viewpoints and Composition offer a way to *collectively* address the questions that arise during rehearsal. Actors, freed from seeking parental approval, are given responsibility as co-creators of the event. Viewpoints and Composition shift the tables so that every participant must find a compelling reason to be in the room, to have a stake in the process, and to claim ownership in the outcome.

Some gifts we receive from Viewpoints.

Surrender

Viewpoints relieves the pressure to have to invent by yourself, to generate all alone, to be interesting and force creativity. Viewpoints allows us to surrender, fall back into empty creative space and trust that there is something there, other than our own ego or imagination, to catch us. Viewpoints helps us trust in *letting something occur* onstage, rather than *making it occur*. The source for action and invention comes to us from others and from the physical world around us.

Possibility

Viewpoints helps us recognize the limitations we impose on ourselves and our art by habitually submitting to a presumed *absolute authority*, be it the text, the director, the teacher. It frees us from the statement: "My character would never do that." In Viewpoints, there is no good or bad, right or wrong—there is only possibility and, later in the process, *choice*.

Choice and Freedom

Viewpoints leads to greater *awareness*, which leads to greater *choice*, which leads to greater *freedom*. Once you are aware of a full spectrum, you do not need to choose all of it all the time, but you are *free* to, and you are no longer bound by unconsciousness. Range increases. You can begin to paint with greater variety and mastery.

Growth

Viewpoints becomes a personal litmus test, a gauge for your own strengths and weaknesses, for discovering how you are free and how you are inhibited, what your own patterns and habits are. Again it is *awareness* that offers us this gift—the option to change and grow.

Wholeness

Viewpoints awakens all our senses, making it clear how much and how often we live only in our heads and see only through our eyes. Through Viewpoints we learn to listen with our entire bodies and see with a sixth sense. We receive information from levels we were not even aware existed, and begin to communicate back with equal depth.

CHAPTER 4

HOW TO BEGIN?

PHYSICAL REQUIREMENTS

A sprung-wood floor is optimal for Viewpoints. Concrete and carpeted surfaces are not good for the knees and other joints. Make sure that the surface is clean and smooth with no dangerous sharp protrusions or cracks. Remove all excess furniture from the room or hall and, if possible, find an alternate space to store people's personal belongings. The attention to cleanliness and order will contribute to a good working environment.

Participants should be barefoot. Sneakers are second best when there are reasons for not being barefoot. But in either case make sure the group's footwear is not mixed. If barefoot, socks should definitely be removed because of the danger of slippage. Clothing should not restrict movement. Hair should be pulled back and jewelry removed.

Start on time. Beginning and ending work sessions with punctuality shows a respect for one another and adds a sense of order which, paradoxically, allows for more complexity and abandon inside the allotted time.

Everyone accepts responsibility for her/his individual safety and the safety of the group. This responsibility is shared. People's safety should not be put in danger: make sure that people aren't throwing themselves around carelessly, that they respect any past injuries. Bruises should not result from this work.

"If you can't say it, point to it."

In order to introduce the basic concepts behind Viewpoints, it is necessary to move through certain fundamental exercises, which are very difficult to talk about. As the Austrian philosopher Ludwig Wittgenstein wrote: "If you can't say it, point to it." The following exercises "point to" important principles that are best understood through doing rather than describing. Encourage the participants to savor the experience of the exercises and do the best they can in every moment. Explain that the crucial issues will be reviewed verbally only at the end of the session.

EXERCISE 1: RUNNING STRETCHES

The first session involves quite a bit of running and jumping, so it is wise to do a series of leg stretches to loosen up.

1. Stand in a circle. Start with the feet about shoulder distance apart and turn the toes slightly inward. Drop the head down and allow the arms to hang loose. With each exhalation allow another tension held in the body to release. As the breaths go by, the releasing reaches deeper and into smaller muscles. Exhale four times.
2. Together, everyone brings their right leg back, keeping both legs straight, heels remaining on the ground. Hang the top of your body over the left leg, still focusing on another four exhalations.

3. Drop the right knee down about two inches off the ground, releasing the muscles of the right thigh. Keep the left heel on the floor and, again, focus on four exhales. Try to remain present, in the room, without haste or hurry. Next, drop the elbows to the floor keeping the right knee off the floor and the left heel down. Again, breathe.

4. Come back up, elbows off the ground, place the right knee on the floor, take hold of the right ankle with the left hand, open the chest and reach out with the free right arm. Relax the shoulders. Breathe.

5. Finally, go backward through the previous positions, four exhalations each position, until everyone is, once again, with both feet shoulder distance apart, head hanging over. Do the same series of exercises on the opposite side of the body, starting with the left leg back.

6. At the end, roll up the spine. Everyone is still in a smooth circle, with equal space between each person. With *soft focus* everyone in the circle should be visible to one another.

   Note: *Soft focus* is explained in greater detail later in this chapter. Briefly, *soft focus* is a physical state in which the eyes are relaxed so that, rather than looking *at* a specific object or person, the individual allows visual information to *come to* her/him. With focus softened in the eyes, the individual expands the range of awareness, especially peripherally. We teach and practice all beginning Viewpoints using *soft focus*.

EXERCISE 2: SUN SALUTATIONS

The sun salutations are derived from yoga. In the traditional yoga practice the focus is internal. In our training, the focus of each individual is on the whole group. It is important to learn to sense the consent of the group as a whole and learn to enjoy unison movement. No individual is leading and no individual is following. It is vital to cultivate wakefulness and a collective, shared present.

The twelve sun salutations are performed in unison. To start, the salutations should be quite slow, then gradually get faster. After each sun salutation, the group inhales and exhales together once before going on to the next (except for the final three, which have no breath in between). The most important thing to keep in mind, besides doing the exercises safely, is to stay together, in unison. Applying *soft focus* throughout the whole exercise encourages each participant's peripheral vision and full body to listen; qualities so essential to Viewpoints training.

1. Stand in a circle, each individual visible to everyone else in the group. Maintain *soft focus* and an awareness of everyone else's positioning. Feet are parallel, shoulder distance apart. Both palms are touching in front of the chest.

2. At the same moment everyone begins to move the palms, still touching directly upward. When a point is reached where the hands cannot remain together any longer the hands separate. Everyone in the circle opens her/his hands at the same instant. The arms continue to rise to the full extent directly upward. Then everyone together bends the upper body backward, careful not to squeeze the lower spine.

3. The upper body then, back remaining straight and arms on either side of the ears, slowly descends in front of the body until both hands are fully on the floor on either side of the feet. It is all right for the knees to be bent in this position. Again, this is accomplished simultaneously with everyone else in the circle. *Soft focus* and listening to the whole are necessary.

4. Keeping your hands on the floor, and with head facing out, extend either leg behind you into a lunge position with the knee touching down. The heel of the forward foot remains flat on the floor. Everyone takes her/his hands off the ground at the same instant and bends backward, opening the chest. After a few moments, touch the hands down again.

5. Next, move the forward leg back to join the other. Now raise the buttocks upward as you extend the chest and heels

of both feet downward. In yoga, this position is known as *downward facing dog*.

6. The knees start to descend directly down to the floor. Everyone moves the knees at the same instant and all knees touch the floor at the same instant. Now both hands and both knees support you.

7. The torso moves down and through until it reaches upward into a backward bending *cobra* position. The head remains straight forward.

8. And now move in reverse through the last six moves (steps 2–7). The toes tuck under and the arms push back once again into *downward facing dog*. Now everyone moves backward through the same series of moves until the whole circle is standing with hands in front of the chest. During all these moves, the challenge is to flow through the positions without stopping while also attempting to move in unison. Once the group is back in the original position (palms touching in front of chest, etc.), the spacing and integrity of the circle should be reconfirmed. Then everyone breathes together once in and once out, and then begins together the next sun salutation, this time a bit faster.

Remember: at the end of the first nine sun salutations, the group takes a communal inhalation and exhalation. The last three are done with no breath in between.

The group collaborates on an acceleration of speed during the twelve sun salutations. In addition to staying in unison and building the speed together, this exercise cultivates a sense of individual freedom inside a set form. The group should grow sensitive to the little communal charges of energy that occur from the shared physical engagement.

The last three sun salutations, done at an increasingly quick speed, will challenge the group (and each individual) to work even harder to stay together. It is important that the final salutation ends with everyone hitting the final position at the same instant.

EXERCISE 3: HIGH JUMPS

Still standing in a circle, the group jumps in place together, as high as possible. The jump is not initiated by any individual but, rather, happens because of a shared consent. The goal is to simultaneously jump as high as possible, to land together in the same instant, and to land on the floor with as little noise as possible. At the height of the jump the feet should be tucked up under the buttocks so that as much space between the floor and the body as possible can be achieved. This exercise should be repeated until the group has discovered together how to accomplish the task.

EXERCISE 4: FIVE IMAGES

While running in place, still in a circle, introduce a series of five images (see list below), one at a time. The participants should try to visualize each image as fully as possible in their bodies. Finally, all five images should be experienced simultaneously.

1. Imagine a beautiful golden band around your head pulling gently upward.
2. Use *soft focus*.
3. Loosen your arms and shoulders.
4. Imagine that your legs are strong and muscular and that your bare feet are accustomed to working in the soil. Feel the sense of descent into the ground.
5. Place your hands on your heart. Find the beating of the heart. Extend the arms outward and imagine working with an open heart.

Repeat these instructions so that all five images are present at the same time (the fifth image can now exist without touching the heart or gesturing outward).

This exercise is a reminder that the body forms a line between heaven and earth, a line that unites the two. Encourage the participants to return to these images whenever they become exhausted or confused.

EXERCISE 5: RUN TO CENTER

Form a very wide circle facing inward and begin running in place. One person can at any moment initiate a run into the center of the space (make sure that feet are not stepped on). In that split second of initiation, everyone should run toward the center together in such a way that someone watching would not be able to tell who initiated. After everyone has run to the center, everyone should run backward to reestablish the wide circumference of the circle.

After some repetition of this exercise, each participant will experience firsthand that anything can happen at any time and that s/he needs to be completely present in the moment, ready to move in response to stimuli.

Repeat this exercise until the group is successfully communicating moment to moment.

EXERCISE 6: TWELVE/SIX/FOUR

This exercise cultivates listening and responding in the moment both individually and as a group.

Everyone runs in a circle in the same direction at the same speed. The space between individuals in the circle should be equidistant, maintained by each person constantly gauging the spatial distance behind and in front of them. With *soft focus*, each participant is simultaneously aware of the person in front and the person behind *as well as the entire group*.

Introduce the following three options:

1. Without any one individual initiating, the entire group finds a way to *change direction* at the same instant. Everyone should turn toward the inside of the circle when changing direction. It is important that the group does not slow down to make these changes easier. Turning should be precise and succinct. The group should look for a mutual consent to act together.

2. While running in a circle an individual within the group initiates a *jump*. Whoever initiates should jump very high

so that the rest of the group has the opportunity to join in. At the moment that the individual jumps, everyone jumps with her/him, and everyone lands on the ground at the same instant and stays crouched down. Then the whole group looks for mutual consent to continue, and together all begin to run in the *opposite direction*.

3. An individual in the group also initiates this third option, a sudden *stop*, while the group is running in a circle. In the moment that the person stops, everyone stops. This event of stopping should be instantaneous, coefficient and exhilarating. From the stillness after the stop, the group looks for mutual consent to continue running, at which point the running resumes in the *same direction* as before.

Once these three options have been introduced, the group should be given the task of completing twelve changes of direction, six jumps, and four stops in any order. Remember: the changes are not initiated by an individual, they emerge from group consent; the jumps and stops *are* originated by individuals in the group. Someone on the outside should keep count. It's best to count backward so that occasionally s/he will call out, for example: "Six changes, two jumps and three stops remaining."

Almost as much can be learned by watching this activity as doing it. If there are enough participants, divide into two or three smaller groups, so that everyone can both see and do it.

This exercise illustrates the necessity for the entire body to listen in each moment. We often assume that we are listening, but the Twelve/Six/Four exercise reveals how demanding that task actually is and how shut off we normally are from one another onstage.

EXERCISE 7: THE CHASE

As soon as the group finishes the Twelve/Six/Four exercise, they should stand still in the circle with equal space between each participant. Indicate the direction the circle will move and then ask each person to imagine a compelling reason why s/he would want to touch the back of the person in front of them. Then each should find an equally compelling reason not to get touched from behind. Then ask each participant to raise the stakes in her/his desire to touch the person ahead and not get touched from behind. Everyone should be in a state of *feedforward*, in which the attention is focused outward in anticipation, and prepared to move on command (see "Feedforward and Feedback" at the end of this chapter). Say: "Go." The participants try to touch the person ahead of them and not get touched from behind, without making the circle any smaller and with no vocal sound. If someone does manage to touch a person's back then they should try to maintain gentle contact.

Do not allow this exercise to exceed ten seconds following any: "Go." After the first try, the group changes direction and each goes after the person who has been pursuing them.

This exercise cultivates an appetite for the thrilling fiction of a chase. It helps push the group movement into a full body activity rather than a theoretical exercise.

EXERCISE 8: PERIPHERAL VISION

After Exercises 5–7, which include full-out running, ask everyone to walk freely in a space experiment with *presence*. Presence is related to personal moment-to-moment *interest*; interest is something that cannot be faked or indicated. Everyone should use *soft focus* in order to develop awareness of the group and the surrounding space. The participants walk continuously throughout this exercise. While walking, have them refer back to the sense imagery of Exercise 4: the sensation of the golden band pulling up, the *soft focus*, strong legs and feet, open heart. This will be helpful.

Next, each participant chooses one person in the group to observe without letting that person know that they are being studied. Use *soft focus*, do not look directly at the chosen person, rather, see them in the periphery of your vision. Do not let the selected individual go out of your field of vision at any time.

Allow information about the selected person to *come toward* you. You are reversing the habitual way information is processed. Rather than reaching out for information, let the information come to you. With *soft focus*, notice the color of the person's clothes and skin, their unique shape, the rhythm of their walk, etc. Be aware of the moment when you lose interest, the moment that you stop allowing new information in. Attempt to remain present and interested in the information (the news) about this person.

After about a minute of this *soft focus* observation of an individual, ask everyone to release that person from her/his view. Each participant should choose a new person, again watched in the same *soft*, surreptitious way, with the task of allowing the differences to be discerned and felt. The information, or news, of this person's difference from the previous person should be noticed. The colors are different, the body is different, and the tempos are different.

After a minute or so, ask each person to add another individual to her/his peripheral vision without losing track of the one already under observation. Now there are two people in each person's peripheral vision. At no time should one of those two people leave the field of vision. Now with twice as much *news* to feel and experience, ask the participants not to clump the two people together in their minds, but rather to allow for the differences of the two people to have their effect. After a while, add yet another person into the peripheral vision, so now the same three remain in the field of vision, all three allowed to remain distinct and individual. After a while add a fourth. The same four people should always remain in the person's field of vision. If it is possible, add a fifth. Finally, let all five go and ask everybody to return to just walking with *presence* and *interest*.

Finally, ask everyone to choose a new person to observe with *soft focus*. Next, each participant should walk directly *toward* that person and come to a stop as close as possible to her/him. It will happen often that the group will fold into one or two subgroups. Once all the participants are still, ask them to close their eyes. Remind the group that there are many sources for information besides seeing. Touch, for example, and sound and smell, and the sensation of heat or cold. Information seeps into the body through many places. Ask the participants to locate a part of their perceptual system that is not eager to be present and receptive. For example, perhaps a foot is pulled away, or a shoulder tensed. Ask them to include this part of their body in the sensation of the moment. Ask them to allow themselves to receive information—*news*—from all senses. After a minute or two, ask them to open their eyes without allowing vision to dominate the other senses. Have the participants move away from each other, all the while maintaining their sense of openness and heightened sensory perception.

We'd like to *point to* a few crucial issues that the training and these eight exercises have already touched upon.

Soft focus.

Soft focus is the physical state in which we allow the eyes to soften and relax so that, rather than looking at one or two things in sharp focus, they can now take in many. By taking the pressure off the eyes to be the dominant and primary information gatherer, the whole body starts to listen and gather information in new and more sensitized ways.

In a culture governed by commodities, consumption and the glorification of the individual, we are taught to target what we want and then find a way to get it. The way we use our eyes in daily life entails looking for what might satisfy our particular desires. When we are hungry, for example, we only see bakeries. We stroll past stores and restaurants mostly looking at what we want to buy or who we want to have. Like a hunter after prey, our vision is narrowed down to a preconceived series of possibilities.

In Viewpoints training, the participants are asked to look at the surroundings and at other people *without* desire. Exercise 8 reverses our habitual, acculturated ways of looking and seeing. It encourages *soft focus*, allowing the world in. It develops a global perception. The exercise asks us not to go *out* toward what we want, searching for prey, but rather, with *soft focus*, to reverse our habitual directional focus and allow information to move *in* toward us. News *penetrates* our sensibilities. When the eyes, which tend to dominate the senses, are softened, the other senses are given equal value.

When you cannot see
What is happening,
Do not stare harder.
Relax and look gently
With your inner eye.

—LAO TZU

The development of an artist is related to her/his ability to perceive differences. As children, we quickly categorize the world into big clumps, for example: houses, people, streets. Categorizing the world makes it a safer place, because through it we tame the untamed world around us. All things, once categorized, become less threatening to us, and can be safely filed away. Untaming the world and allowing the differences between people and between streets and houses to be felt and acknowledged mark the growth of an artist. The capacity to differentiate moment to moment is an actor's most basic and crucial skill.

Extraordinary listening.

To work effectively in the theater, a field that demands intense collaboration, the ability to listen is the defining ingredient. And yet, it is very difficult to listen—to really listen. Through Viewpoints training, we learn to listen with the whole body, with the entire being. Until you experience listening with the whole body, you do not realize what a rare occurrence it actually is.

Ask the participants to remember the sensation of the moment when the group found the consent to change direction, while running together in a circle during the Twelve/Six/Four exercise. Point out that this sensibility of alertness, quickness, availability and openness to one another, and the sense that anything might happen, is necessary in each instant of Viewpoints. We normally assume that we are listening when in fact we are preoccupied. Listening involves the entire body in relation to the ever-changing world around us. In Viewpoints training, one learns to listen with the entire body.

In Viewpoints training, as in rehearsal, if one is always looking for a particular premeditated result, then many things that are happening outside of those parameters are not recognized. Extraordinary listening means listening with the whole body without an idea of the result. When something happens in the room, everybody present can respond instantly, bypassing the frontal lobe of the brain in order to act upon instinct and intuition.

Ongoing awareness of others in time and space.

Much of this early training involves keeping everyone together in Time and Space. While running in a circle, an attempt is made to maintain equal space between people: this is an example of keeping together in Space. When someone jumps everyone tries to land simultaneously: this is an example of keeping together in Time. These exercises are meant to teach the importance of an intense awareness of what other people are doing, where they are and when they are doing it. Many of these early exercises are performed in unison. This unison work represents the ABCs of Viewpoints training. Once you are able to move truly in unison with others, you can start to work with more advanced concepts of counterpoint, juxtaposition and contrast.

Feedforward and feedback.

This preliminary session introduced two poles of experience and energy that need to be calibrated and sharpened: *feedforward* and *feedback*.

Feedforward is an outgoing energy that anticipates the necessity for action. Playing volleyball, for example, demands an intense use of *feedforward* as the ball whizzes around the space.

Feedback is the information and sensation that one receives as the result of an action. Whereas, in a sporting event, the energy of *feedforward* is predominantly what the onlookers connect to, in a theater event it is also the energy of *feedback* that engages us. As a viewer in a sports arena, we will most likely be interested in the anticipation of the next action. As a viewer in the theater, not only are we caught up in that suspense but additionally, and even more powerfully, we invest in the event through our empathy with the actors' experience. Through our identification with this experience, the theater becomes a place of acute aliveness to both the drama of what *has* happened and to what *will* happen next.

CHAPTER 5

INTRODUCING THE INDIVIDUAL VIEWPOINTS

The individual Viewpoints should be introduced separately, with most, if not all, of the participant's attention on the specifically named Viewpoint.

You'll find overlaps and connections between the separate Viewpoints. An especially open group of participants will often jump ahead or add on even before you've introduced the next Viewpoint. This happens naturally, of course, because Viewpoints is already in the body. Slowing the process down and forcing the group to maintain conscious focus during the beginning stages produces greater range and finesse later on. If too many View-points are layered on too quickly no single one can ever be explored with enough depth.

As each Viewpoint is individually introduced, information accumulates. First, we isolate awareness of that particular View-point, then add another to it. Each Viewpoint is, in turn, dealt with on its own terms, then added to what has already been investigated.

Learning the individual Viewpoints is like learning to juggle. First there is only one ball in the air, then a second is added, then a third, a fourth, and so on—how many balls can you keep in the air before they all drop? When introducing the individual Viewpoints, pay attention to when the balls start to drop. You might discover that a group of participants needs to practice a particular Viewpoint over time before it is able to add another without completely losing awareness of the first.

At the same time, it is most effective to introduce most, if not all, Viewpoints in a single session. Rather than getting stuck on any one Viewpoint, allow the first session to be messy and confusing and exhilarating and overwhelming. Go back to the basics of the individual Viewpoints in the first several sessions after the group has gleaned an overall sense of how Viewpoints works.

TEMPO

Tempo is a good Viewpoint with which to begin when introducing Viewpoints individually.

In working on Tempo the focus is not on *what* the action is but on *how fast* or *slow* the action is performed: awareness of *speed*. To work on Tempo in isolation, you can choose almost any action (extending an arm, waving to someone, turning your head) and experiment with performing it in different tempos.

EXERCISE 1: TEMPO, THE BASICS

1. Choose one action, with a clear beginning and end.
2. Repeat it several times, making sure the form is exact and repeatable.
3. Perform the action in a medium tempo.
4. Perform the action in a fast tempo.
5. Perform the action in a slow tempo.

Be aware of how the action of changing tempos alters the meaning of the physical action. For example, I am sitting at a table and I reach my right hand out about a foot across the table. (Most actions, when initially performed without thought or context, will occur in a *medium* tempo. So let's say this is the tempo at which I extend my hand.) I then perform the same action *fast*. Then *slow*. What verbs are implied by performing the same action at different speeds? The *medium* perhaps implies "to touch" or "to retrieve," whereas the *fast* action is maybe "to grab" or "to protect," and the *slow* maybe "to seduce" or "to sneak." Similarly, the *fast* tempo makes me feel desperate, the *slow* makes me feel scared, and the *medium* makes me feel . . . well, nothing at all. This is one of the gifts of Viewpoints: by applying each Viewpoint, especially in its extremes, we *invite* something to happen.

As with all the Viewpoints, Tempo can be practiced both for its own sake (to increase awareness and range of Tempo) or as a tool to increase overall expressivity or jump-start a moment or scene. It's like someone who lifts weights in the gym—he might increase the weight simply for the sake of it, or he might increase the weight so that he can lift heavier objects at home or work. A performer might practice faster and faster tempos so that when s/he is onstage s/he can call on that tempo with more consciousness and ease.

EXERCISE 2: SWITCHES OF TEMPO

This exercise will help increase the individual's awareness of the *extremes* of Tempo, in which s/he might not ordinarily operate. It will expand range and develop the individual's ability to shift in and out of extreme tempos instantly and unexpectedly.

1. Have the group stand in a circle (this is Topography, a Viewpoint of Space). Each person should be an arm's length apart from the person on either side (this is Spatial Relationship, another Viewpoint of Space). Make sure the group is in *soft focus*. Perhaps do some simple movement exercises

in unison (lifting an arm together, leaning, etc.) to focus
concentration.

2. The group should lean gently from one foot to the other. At
   this point, assuming you have done a unison group warm-
   up, allow the group to let go of unison focus and concentrate solely on the individual body and their own sense of
   Tempo. Each person should shift her/his weight from foot
   to foot in her/his own time now.

3. With an awareness of both Viewpoints (Shape and Tempo),
   gradually begin to increase both: a knee begins to bend,
   then lift that same leg so that a walking motion is created,
   then shift from foot to foot, leg to leg, getting faster until
   you find yourself in a nice, comfortable, *medium* tempo,
   jogging in place. Maintain *soft focus*. Keep breathing.
   Through your *soft focus*, know exactly where you are in the
   room, on the floor, and in relationship to those around
   you. Spot yourself. The tendency while running in place in
   a circle will be for the group to constantly move in and
   close down the circle. Staying in *soft focus*, find physical
   landmarks in the space to help you remain in a fixed place.
   Call this your *medium* tempo. It's what feels *in the middle*
   (comfortable) for you. Remember it by observing how it
   makes you feel, breathe, see. You will return to it.

   Note: Very often as you begin work in *soft focus* and
   are addressing the group, certain individuals will look at
   you as soon as you begin speaking—the lure of language is
   powerful. Remind the group, or individuals, of *soft focus* as
   often as necessary.

4. Explain to the group that you will be adding tempos to
   both sides of the *medium* tempo, gradually increasing the
   ends of the spectrum. When you clap your hands, the
   group should shift into a tempo called *slow*. Then, on the
   next clap, switch back to *medium*. With the next clap, add a
   fast tempo. Then clap again, and back to *medium*: *soft focus*,
   breathe, maintain the circle.

5. Now add two more tempos to the *slow* side of the spectrum.
   Call them *very slow* and *the slowest you can go and still call it*

movement. With claps, switch unexpectedly to different tempos, in different orders, and stay in those tempos for varying lengths of time (this is Duration, a Viewpoint of Time). Then add two more tempos on the *fast* side of the spectrum: *very fast* and *hyper-speed. Hyper-speed* should be pushed so that people are running in place as fast—but as light—as they can.

When working in *fast* tempos, balance on the inside by maintaining a sense of calm, quiet, *slow.* This is similar to the emphasis placed on control and ease when performing fight choreography. Each action contains itself and *its opposite.* Practice running *fast on the outside* and *slow on the inside.* Then switch to *slow on the outside* and *fast on the inside.* When you decrease the tempo, do not let the energy decrease.

EXERCISE 3: TEMPO ON A GRID

1. The group runs in a *medium* jog. On a hand clap, they turn to their right and run in a circle. They are now traveling through space instead of running in place. Maintain a constant distance between bodies. With *soft focus*, be aware of the entire group, the entire circle, become aware that the circle is a Topography.

2. With the next hand clap, the group switches out of the circle to work on a new Topography—a *grid.* Imagine a series of straight lines, crisscrossing each other at ninety-degree angles on the ground, like a giant piece of graph paper on the floor. The angles correspond to the walls of the room, eliminating all curves and diagonals. With this next hand clap, the group now moves anywhere along the lines of this imagined grid on the floor. They do not need to stay together in a group; individuals are free to explore the grid in any direction.

3. Keep your focus on Tempo—how fast you are going. Continuing to work on the grid and in *soft focus*, begin to add *switches* of tempo at your own will. Individuals are now

working on their own, simply moving along the grid in various patterns and at various tempos. Notice if there are tempos you stay away from or resist—then add them! Include *hyper-speed* and *the slowest you can go and still call it movement.* Notice when you get bored. What do you have to do to surprise yourself? As you continue working on the grid with switches of tempo, it is useful to add awareness of another Viewpoint: Duration.

DURATION

Tempo asks you to be aware of *how fast* you perform an action; Duration asks you to be aware of *how long* you stay in that action and/or tempo. In reaching your hand out in a *very slow* tempo you might choose to stay in it for three seconds or ten. Or, following one of Pinter's stage-direction pauses, how do you know when to speak the next line or let the silence sit another three beats? Practicing Duration increases the performer's ability to sense how long is long enough to make something happen onstage and, conversely, how long is too long so that something starts to die.

In introducing Duration, it is helpful to choose one action that remains constant (in this case, moving on a grid), used in conjunction with switches of tempo, so that the individual does not need to concentrate on *what* s/he is doing, only on *how long.*

EXERCISE 4: DURATION AND TEMPO ON THE GRID

Now that the group has been working on the grid with switches of tempo, ask the participants to become aware of patterns that are emerging. Not only which tempos they tend to rely on or ignore, but also how often they are switching tempos. Note aloud to the group that almost everyone is probably switching her/his tempo regularly, rhythmically, and in short bursts. This is a standard, fallback position when it comes to Duration.

As with all the individual Viewpoints, we tend to live in a *medium* area with Duration, a gray zone, in which things last a comfortable, average, seemingly coherent amount of time. We tend to shy away from things that last *very long*, or change very quickly, i.e., *very short.*

With this in mind, work on the grid, continuing with changes of tempo, but putting ninety percent of your focus on Duration now. Stay in tempos longer than feels comfortable, or shorter. As you move on the grid now, you are experimenting not only with how fast you go but how long you stay in each speed.

Be aware of a kind of Morse code that you are creating over time—longer dashes, shorter dots. Interest yourself. Surprise yourself. Meaning is created over time by how different durations are combined with each other: Loooooooooooong-short-short-short! Medium-medium-medium-medium-short-medium.

To expand on the above:

1. After adding changes of tempo and duration, add *changes of direction* on the grid. Now people can move forward, backward or sideways.
2. Add *changes of levels*, so that the grid in the mind's eye is not two-dimensional on the floor, but three-dimensional in space. Now people can travel on tiptoe, as high as possible, or in a crawl or slither, as low as possible. Make sure that focus stays on Tempo and Duration and that, in adding awareness of vertical space and different ways of traveling, people do not become engaged in playing with Shape.
3. Add *stops* and *starts.*
4. For a time, forget everything but *top speed* and *stillness.* Those are the only two choices. Devour space with no fear. See through your back. Keep the inside and outside energy balancing each other, so that you work with a sense of inner calm and slowness when you are traveling at hyper-speed, and a sense of inner momentum when you are traveling slowly.
5. You, as group leader, will be able tell if someone has predetermined where they are going to stop or when they are

going to start. Point this out. Say: "I can see where you're going to stop because you've already decided." Keep reminding them to surprise themselves.

KINESTHETIC RESPONSE

EXERCISE 5: INTRODUCING KINESTHETIC RESPONSE ON THE GRID

Continuing to work with *stops* and *starts* on the grid, start to shift the bulk of your focus away from Tempo and Duration and toward Kinesthetic Response. Kinesthetic Response is your spontaneous physical reaction to movement outside yourself. Put your focus on other bodies in the space, and let your stops and starts be determined by *them*. Let the decision to move or be still be made by when others affect you, when they pass you, start around you, stop around you, etc. In focusing on Kinesthetic Response, you are now working on *when* you move rather than *how fast* (Tempo) or *how long* (Duration).

A crucial moment in Viewpoints training.

Until this moment, individuals have been playing with Tempo and Duration in their own way on the grid. This is the moment when we introduce the imperative of relinquishing choice (at least for the moment). It is no longer for you to choose what is right or wrong, good or bad—but to *use everything*. If someone runs by you—use it! If the group suddenly shifts into slow motion—use it! Let everything change you. Although this is one of the most difficult stages of the process, it can also be the most freeing. This is the moment when you take the onus off the individual to "be interesting," to "be inventive," to "come up with stuff." If the individual is open, listens with her/his whole body, sees the world through *soft focus*, s/he need only receive and react.

This is Kinesthetic Response (a Viewpoint of Time): the imme-diate, uncensored response to an external event around you.

REPETITION

EXERCISE 6: INTRODUCING REPETITION ON THE GRID

Next, focus on Repetition. Let when you move (Kinesthetic Response), how you move (Tempo) and for how long you move (Duration) be determined by Repetition.

1. Let go of thinking about Tempo, Duration and Kinesthetic Response. Concentrate on Repetition. All your movement now should be determined by repeating someone else, either their path, their direction, their speed, their stops and starts, etc. Follow someone, shadow her/him. Don't get caught with one person. Constantly switch to a new person as s/he comes into your field of play.
2. Practice repeating off someone far away from you as well as someone near you.
3. Now repeat off two people instead of just one. Work with repetition of one person's *floor pattern* and another person's tempo.
4. Make use of your *awareness* of Repetition over time, so that you can now recycle and incorporate movement that occurred earlier in the exercise. Let yourself be carried away, thrown around the grid, bounced between other bodies, repeating *everything* that you see and hear, with your *soft focus* and by listening through your back, so that you are using movement that is occurring on all sides of you, not just in front.

SPATIAL RELATIONSHIP

EXERCISE 7: INTRODUCING SPATIAL RELATIONSHIP ON THE GRID

1. The group moves on the grid, relaxing attention, letting instinct carry them, rather than being guided by one particular Viewpoint. Allow this to go on for a minute or two, or until the group is moving freely and naturally, without imposing ideas on their movement patterns. Clap your hands to have the group stop, to hold in stillness.

2. Ask the participants to notice the space between themselves and others. The distance between bodies. This is Spatial Relationship. Ask them to notice how even all the space is (which it will more or less be at this point in the training).

    As we've noted before while introducing other Viewpoints, we tend to operate in a space which is very middle-of-the-road, without extremes, with great safety and comfort. In Spatial Relationship this translates to a consistency of distance between bodies, usually two to five feet. This is the distance from others in which we spend most of our lives. It's the distance we have while chatting, when shaking hands, when eating a meal. We tend to keep this cushion of space as protection, and when we start to increase or decrease this space, we start to create dynamic, event, *relationship*.

3. With your next clap, the group begins moving on the grid again, at ninety-degree angles—this time working with an acute awareness of the space. Let them know that this time they should let themselves make decisions about when and where to go based only on where other people are. They should work in the extremes of going either *close to* or *far away from* others. Try to work spontaneously. Change as other people change around you.

4. Stop the group again with a clap. Notice how the spatial relationships in the group have changed: they are more interesting, more noticeable, more potent. Something begins to occur in space when we pay attention to it.

5. After introducing individual Viewpoints on the grid, you can do exercises that combine Viewpoints or ingredients in various ways while working on the grid:

- Work on the grid with only *hyper-speed* or *stillness*. Run with no fear. Run with abandon. Run with trust.
- Work on the grid with *level* and Spatial Relationship.
- Work on the grid with only *hyper-speed* or *stillness*, incorporating levels and Spatial Relationship, etc.

You can give structure in any combination that you assess is most challenging or helpful for the particular group.

TOPOGRAPHY

Transition from the Grid: Introducing Topography

1. BASIC PATTERNS. Introduce Topography by pointing out that the grid is itself a topography, that the group already has been working with Topography. Now change the image of the grid into a series of circles. Work on curves and swirls. Change from circles to zigzags or diagonals.

   While working on the grid you may have introduced *levels*—asking the group to imagine the grid as not just two-dimensional (the floor only), but three-dimensional, going up and into the room as an imaginary structure. With this image in mind, the group can explore *height* and *depth* on the grid, working in a topography which is a multidimensional landscape rather than solely a floor pattern.

2. PAINTING ON THE FLOOR. Let the grid dissolve below your feet, and in its place imagine a new topography of your own creation. (At this point, each individual needs to let go of the group focus and turn to a solo focus.) Imagine that the soles of your feet have red paint on them, and you are

now painting the floor. Create various topographies by *painting* on the floor. Work in constantly shifting combinations of circles and zigzags and straight lines.

3. SIZE OF CANVAS. Return to one basic floor pattern for a moment. Maintain this exact pattern while changing the *size* of it. If you've been working with small circles, expand them to take up the whole room; if you've been traversing across the entire floor, use the same floor pattern to work in miniature on a single corner, etc.

4. SHAPE OF CANVAS. Next, add an awareness of *shape* of playing space. If you are working in a corner, actually define it on the floor for yourself with an invisible boundary. Work inside of a square. Or work inside of a circle in the center of the room. Or work inside of an oblong on the farthest downstage edge of the playing space (we often refer to this extreme downstage area as *in one*, a term derived from vaudeville). You are now working with *pattern* itself, *size* of pattern and *shape* of playing space.

As you work with *shape* of playing space, *size* of playing space and *pattern within* playing space, change one but maintain the other two. For instance, if you are working with zigzags, do so within a small square. Now change floor pattern to become circles within the circle. Now maintain the pattern (i.e., the circles), but change the shape of the playing space, i.e., making circles within a triangle. Now change the size of the playing space by enlarging the triangle to reach into three corners of the room.

In the beginning it is often necessary, when working on Topography, for the group to maintain a ten-percent awareness on Tempo. The natural inclination of any group will be to work on Topography in a *fast* but *easy* tempo (just as we will discover later that it is natural to at first work on Shape in a *slow* tempo). By working on Topography in a *very fast* or *slow* tempo, new patterns will emerge.

If you need to take a break, you could do it at this stage in the process, before introducing the Viewpoints of Shape, Gesture and Architecture. Make sure that you do not take too long a break before finishing the introduction of all the Viewpoints and putting them together in either Open Viewpoints or Lane Work (both of which are described in detail in the following chapter). A two- or five-minute refresher (allowing people to use the bathroom or get a drink of water) is fine, but a fifteen-minute break, allowing time to cool down and/or revert to being in one's head, is not. It is very useful in the first sessions of Viewpoints training to *push* the group—to lead them into a state of heightened and demanding physicality and mental concentration.

SHAPE

EXERCISE 8: INTRODUCING SHAPE, THE BASICS

1. LINES. Everyone stands alone somewhere in the space, focusing on her/his body, beginning in a neutral, relaxed position (*soft focus*). Become aware that your body is already making a shape, i.e., an outline against space, a silhouette. Get a clear sense of this shape as if against an expanse of sky, or a cyclorama. Remaining in your spot, begin to create new shapes by moving parts of your body, concentrating first on shapes which are *linear* or *angular*. (In painting it is common practice to deconstruct and understand form as a combination of lines and curves.) Make only shapes which include angle, lines, hard edges. Use parts of your body other than just arms and legs: use your elbow, knee, tongue. Continue awareness on *legibility*, i.e., how easy the shape is to *read* from the outside.

2. CURVES. Now take the shapes you are making and translate them into shapes which are *curved* or *circular*. Every shape should now be comprised only of rounded lines and edges. Note the different feeling that is evoked for you by curves instead of angles.

3. COMBINATION. Combine lines and curves in your body by isolating different body parts and having one in a straight line and another in a gentle curve. Experiment with differ-

ent combinations. Create contrast and juxtaposition and tension in your various shapes.

4. FLUIDITY AND SPONTANEITY. Note how you are making a shape, stopping, then starting a new one. Try to keep the movement fluid, so one shape leads to the next, so the process is of one shape *evolving* into another. Let the shape itself lead you, rather than you leading the shape. Next, add changes of tempo and note how different tempos lead to different kinds of shapes. Let the varying tempos kick you into spontaneity; working at a faster tempo will give you less time to predetermine.

5. TRAVELING. Shape can be either stationary or moving. Take the exact shape you are in and begin moving through the space with it, allowing the shape itself to dictate a new, probably unusual, way of traversing space. As you cross the room, allow the shape to evolve. Find new shapes that you can travel in/with.

6. OTHERS. Shape can be created solo or with others. As you travel around the space in Shape, allow contact with other shapes (people in this case). Allow your shapes to merge and shift so that you are now creating *one* shape from two bodies or three bodies.

   At this point, the usual tendency for a group while working on Shape is to turn the shapes inward, becoming a single amorphous blob of slithering bodies. The group will most likely end up on the floor, entangled in each other in an imprecise mass, without legible definition. You will need to point this out, ask them to note it. Encourage them to work with one or two others, making strong, graphic shapes that turn out instead of in.

7. TRAVELING WITH OTHERS. Take the shape you are in with your partner(s) and travel. As you go, allow it to change. As you meet others, disengage from your original shape partner(s) and find yourself in new shapes with new partner(s). Practice *finding yourself* somewhere, in some position, in some shape, without planning it. Allow things to happen. Open up to surprise encounters.

GESTURE

In working on Gesture we will be investigating two categories: Behavioral and Expressive. Behavioral Gestures are those that belong to everyday life, that are part of human behavior as we know and observe it. These are things that people actually do in real life: ways of moving, walking, communicating. Expressive Gestures are those that belong to the interior rather than the exterior world (of behavior); they express feeling or meaning which is not otherwise directly manifest. One could say that Behavioral Gestures are *prosaic* and Expressive Gestures are *poetic*.

EXERCISE 9: EXPRESSIVE GESTURE

1. STARTING. If you are transitioning from the introduction of Shape, it is best to work on Expressive Gesture first. Begin by simply encouraging the group to think of what they are doing no longer as Shape but as Expressive Gesture. What will shift is that we are now working with (1) something *behind* the movement (a feeling, thought, idea); and (2) a beginning, middle and end to the movement.
2. EXPRESSING EMOTIONS. Express something with your gesture. Express a feeling. Make a gesture that expresses a feeling of *joy*. Make a gesture that expresses a feeling of *anger*. Make a gesture that expresses a feeling of *fear*. Make a gesture that expresses a feeling of *sadness*. Move through space with that gesture. Repeat it. Refine it. Let it evolve.
3. EXPRESSING IDEAS. Now work on gestures that express an idea. For instance, express the idea of *freedom* in a movement. Express the concept of *justice*. Now do the same for *war, balance, chaos, the cosmos*.

    It's useful to ask the group to note those parts of the body they tend to rely on, and those they ignore. All nine Viewpoints can serve as a personal litmus test, a method for gauging where the individual's strengths and weaknesses lie, what habits are repeated and what territory is unexplored.

4. USING YOUR WHOLE BODY. Include the parts of your body that you're not used to working with—include all parts of your body. Work from the feet to the head; make an Expressive Gesture first with your toes, then your heels, then your whole foot, then your ankles, etc.

EXERCISE 10: BEHAVIORAL GESTURE

1. STARTING. Take whatever gesture you are in and let it evolve from an Expressive one to a Behavioral one. This means taking something relatively abstract, which you would not normally see someone do, and transforming it into something relatively concrete, which you might likely see someone do on the street, in the home, at the office.

    It is important that as the group is led through generating a mass and variety of gestures in the following steps, that they are pushed to do so quickly, without premeditation or judgment. Undoubtedly, what will emerge from this initial pool of gestures will be full of cliché and stereotype. This is not only okay, it is encouraged. It's important that we begin with exactly who we are, what we think, what we preconceive, rather than some notion we have of who we *should* be and how we *should* think. Once again, if we work spontaneously and honestly, Viewpoints training is an invitation to see ourselves, a gateway to greater consciousness.

2. BODY AND HEALTH. Create gestures that give information about a person's body and physical health. These include wounds, scars, disabilities; responses to/expressions of health and illness, such as a sneeze, yawn, buoyant walk, rolling of the neck, etc.; and reactions to weather, such as shivering, a wipe of sweat, fanning oneself, buttoning up, putting a hand out to feel rain or snow, etc.

3. TIME PERIOD AND CULTURES. Make gestures that belong to a specific period or culture, for instance, gestures that are Elizabethan or Jacobean; gestures that are of the 1920s, the 1950s or 1960s; gestures that are only of "now"; or gestures

that are specific to French, Italian or German cultures. See if specific periods evoke specific tempos, shapes, uses of architecture. For instance, when working on gestures of the 1920s, you might notice how the group moves quickly, in staccato bursts, employs shapes that are more angular than round, etc. Ask the group to note these emerging patterns.

This is an important way in which Viewpoints training can lead directly into the rehearsal process, either when working on an extant text or in generating an original piece. It is the *point-and-name* method for creating a vocabulary for the specific piece (see Chapter 10, Viewpoints in Rehearsal). By *pointing to* and *naming* patterns that emerge from a given theme or subject, you begin to define a specific physical vocabulary for your production according to its specific themes and subject.

4. IDIOSYNCRASIES. Make gestures that tell of a person's eccentricities, quirks, and/or habits: a twitch, a way of scratching, cocking the head, curling the lips, a nose scrunch, a foot tap, an odd bend of the elbow.

5. GENRE. Make gestures that belong to specific genres, for instance:

   □ What are gestures that belong to film noir?
   □ What are gestures that belong to the Western?
   □ What are gestures that belong to slapstick, quiz shows, nineteenth century melodrama, commedia dell'arte, and so on?

6. CONNOTATION. Make a series of gestures that *say* something, that have thought and/or intention behind them. For example, in terms of *intention*, make a gesture that fulfills your *intention* of seducing someone or hurting someone; work on "to entertain" or "to warn" or "to quiet."

   For gestures that have *thought or words* behind them, express the words through Gesture. For example, say the following through Gesture: "Hello," "Screw you," "What's up?" "Come here," "Enough!" etc. Make more gestures.

Communicate. If you allow the group to communicate in a direct fashion with one another through Gesture, remind them of *soft focus* so that the exchange happens through Gesture and without eye contact.

As a variation, and to increase specificity, you can work in greater depth on one or two phrases, playing with degree and relationship. For instance, make a gesture for: "Hello," then repeat this as if to someone you know well, then as if to someone you've never met before. Make new gestures for: "Nice to meet you." Make a gesture that says: "Hiya!" more than just: "Hello." Then, through Gesture, continue with variations of: "Hail," "Welcome," "Greetings!" "Hey there," "'S'up?"

7. USING YOUR WHOLE BODY. Use more parts of your body to generate Behavioral Gestures. Use smaller parts: a finger, a toe, an eyebrow, the corner of your lip.

ARCHITECTURE

EXERCISE 11: INTRODUCING ARCHITECTURE

1. THE FLOOR BENEATH YOUR FEET. Shift your awareness to the architecture which is *already* there, with which you are *already* working (albeit probably unconsciously). We always, in some way large or small, position ourselves in relation to mass: to walls, objects we sit in or stand near or far from, posts we lean on, tables we rest on, space we center ourselves in or find the corners of, etc.

Notice your feet on the ground. Is there any pattern or tape on the floor? Notice the walls and how near or far they are from you. How is the light coming into the room? What is the texture of the wood your hand is on? Become acutely aware of exactly where you are and let this architecture inform your movement. Dance with the room. Let it tell you what to do, where to go, how to move. Let the room determine your shapes, your gestures, your tempos, your topographies.

2. SOLID MASS. Let different solid masses within the space give you movement. Dance off the shape of a chair. Walk along the wall. Climb the ledge. Lean on the pole.

3. TEXTURE. Focus not on the mass and weight and structure of an element, but on its texture—not what it is, but of what it is *made*. If you are working with a mask, become aware of whether it is cloth or metal or wood, whether it is hot or cold—let that inform your tempo, your *size*, etc. Move around the room letting your dance change according to what materials you touch.

4. LIGHT. Dance off the light in the room. Work off the pattern of light fixtures or where the window is. Work with or against light. Move in or out of it. Make shadows.

5. COLOR. Dance off color in the room. Maybe you move to and from spots of red in the room, or your movement is inspired by the color of the clothes that others are wearing. Perhaps red becomes a motif and suggests a story or a theme. At any event, you are practicing sensitivity to patterns of color that are normally overlooked.

6. OBJECTS. Dance with smaller objects or props in the space. Find objects that move, that can travel across the room with you or that open and close: a chair, broom, book, clothing rack, paint can. Move with that object. Develop a relationship with it. Let it taunt you, challenge you, give you an obstacle. Play with it. Turn it into something else. See it and exploit it for its raw qualities rather than its functional ones.

7. INCLUDING OTHERS. Let in the objects that people around you are using—join them. Do not get attached to your own activity to the exclusion of what actually passes in front of your path. Move on to another event in the room . . . and another.

8. THE WHOLE SPACE. At this point the group will most likely still be working within the implicit perimeters of their *playing area*. Encourage them to let in the whole space, not just

a polite and preconceived notion of what is or is not *stage space*. Tell them to break the fourth wall. Go behind the tables. Use the risers, the garbage can, the door to the hall-way. See and include the entirety of the room within which you are working—not just where there is light or empty floor.

9. DISTANT ARCHITECTURE. Shift your focus so that you are no longer working exclusively off the architecture under your feet or in your hand, but also the architecture that is far away, across the room. Dance off the opposite door. Be in dialogue with a distant object.

ENDING THE FIRST BIG SESSION

Gradually reintroduce Viewpoints. You should remind the partic-ipants that they are now working with all the Viewpoints: Archi-tecture, Shape, Gesture, Topography, Kinesthetic Response, Repe-tition, Spatial Relationship, Tempo and Duration. Allow the group to work in Open Viewpoints while occasionally reminding them of the individual Viewpoints they seem to be unaware of. Your coaching can help kick them into a new alive place. Let them work with all the Viewpoints, using the whole space, for ten to fifteen minutes. Then stop them. Ask them to hold where they are, to breathe, be aware of the energy around them, be aware of the Viewpoints, their own Spatial Relationship and Shape, etc. Tell them: "Close your eyes. Become aware of all that you sense through smell, sound, energy." Make them recognize how naturally dom-inant the eyes are, and how much more information there is to take in when they no longer rely on vision. And tell them to *relax*.

Additional Exercises for Focusing on Individual Viewpoints

There are many ways to introduce the individual Viewpoints. Another sequence we have often used is: (1) Spatial Relationship, (2) add Kinesthetic Response, (3) add Tempo, (4) add Duration.

EXERCISE 1: ALTERNATIVE FOR INTRODUCING SPATIAL RELATIONSHIP IN OPEN SPACE

Spatial Relationship is a good Viewpoint to start with on the second or third day of training, or to begin a review session. It simply focuses the individual's attention immediately on the group, on experiencing herself/himself as part of a larger whole. You can start work on Spatial Relationship in an easy, laid-back fashion simply by asking the group to begin moving around the space (with whatever energy they bring in that day). Start where you are, with what you have, become aware of what is happening around you and let that carry you. Remove all pressure to invent or entertain.

EXERCISE 2: FIRST FOCUS—EXTREME DISTANCES

The group moves around the space in any tempo, including *starts* and *stops* (as always, in *soft focus*). Put focus on Spatial Relationship. Notice when you start to feel something happen. Work with more extreme spatial relationships. Go radically close to someone: touch them, hear their breathing, smell them. Then work with someone far away from you: feel the tension, increase it, make the space more taut. In this exercise the only goal is to maintain *extreme* proximity or distance, to live in this state of aliveness, to be sensitive to when it dies and nothing is happening, and start the motor of occurrence again simply by moving closer or farther away from another body.

EXERCISE 3: LINES AND CLUSTERS

Imagine yourself as pinpricks of light, as dots on a Lite Brite set, forming distinct constellations and patterns. Form and dissolve and reform. Make clusters, lines, swirls. If the group at this point is working without strong definition of patterns, encourage them to focus solely on creating lines together, and holding in that particular spatial relationship until everyone is still and they can all feel the spatial relationship. Then ask one person to begin moving, to go anywhere and stop, and others to instantly work off that by moving to a new position, which creates a new line with a new length or diagonal, etc., off the person you asked to move first. You can practice the same thing when creating clusters.

EXERCISE 4: NUMBERS

Continue working on Spatial Relationship by focusing on dynamics created through numbers. Let's say the group has twelve members in it. Ask them to work one against eleven, to move in the space with an awareness of Spatial Relationship but at all times being in a formation of eleven individuals in contrast to one individual (this might mean the eleven go to one side of the room and the one to the other, or it might mean that the eleven form a circle around the one, etc.). You can change the numbers to, for example, six against six, or six pairs of two.

EXERCISE 5: FLOOR PATTERN—EXPRESSING CHARACTER

Think of someone in your life who has a strong stamp, either a strong effect on you or an especially colorful personality. Express her/his *character* in a floor pattern. Is this someone who is very directed and moves in straight lines, or is this someone who is "all over the place" and makes a Jackson Pollock on the floor, or is this someone who likes to take up space, or is this someone who hides in the outskirts? Choose another person and work on expressing her/him, her/his essence as you sense it, in a floor pattern. Choose another. Make sure the three people are clearly differentiated.

EXERCISE 6: FLOOR PATTERN—LIFE STORY

Express the story of your life through a topography. Create a floor pattern which has a journey (a clear beginning, middle and end), and with switches inside of it that correspond to *chapters* of your life: Does your life begin in a small way or a big way? Are your early years linear or circular? Is there a period during which you simply *stop*? Do you go back and repeat patterns? Is there a time during which you shoot unexpectedly ahead? Is there even a clear direction, a goal—or is the path meandering?

Alternative. Have an individual show her/his story. You can then ask members of the group who were watching to tell the story as they perceived it. There is no right or wrong here—it's not a guessing game, but an opportunity to note what was legible, expressive, moving.

Alternative. Have an individual do her/his story while speaking from inside of it, in first-person present tense. S/he does not need to *act*, force events or explain anything. S/he should simply verbalize a stream-of-consciousness, to herself/himself (but loud enough for all to hear), which is anything and everything that comes up with or about that particular *chapter* of life *as s/he is experiencing it*. For example, "I'm so small . . . I'm running around here in this circle because I don't know what anyone wants of me . . . Mommy tells me this . . . Daddy tells me that . . . circle, circle, more circle . . . What?! I'm stopping, I'm stopped—something's changing—look there's a way out . . . I follow it. What is it? A line—I can walk it, I'm going to school now, I know what I'm doing. I can read, I read a lot, I read on this line—whoa! another circle—I'm confused again . . ."

This exercise works well for a group that is just getting to know each other; it offers a way of looking at and discussing a single Viewpoint, but also demands courage on the part of its volunteers and a personalizing of Viewpoints training so that the group immediately learns the emotional, rather than the theoretical, power of the work at hand.

EXERCISE 7: TOPOGRAPHY—AND THE GROUP

Work on creating individual Topography. Add awareness of Tempo and Duration. After some time, add awareness of Repetition (this will lead the group back into a state of working as one again).

Allow individual topographies to change based on what others are giving. Allow topographies to emerge from several (or many) people working as one. Add Kinesthetic Response, so that *when* topographies (direction, pattern, etc.) shift, it is based on something that occurs from the outside (another group or individual).

EXERCISE 8: SHAPE—THE RIVER

Stand in a circle. One person runs into the center of the circle and makes and holds a shape. Another person runs into the center of the circle and adds a shape to the first shape, making a new shape out of both. Add a third person, a fourth, etc., until the whole group has run in and contributed to one overall shape. Choose two or three people to remain in the center and ask everyone else to step out and observe the shape created by those who are left. (The people you choose to keep in the center should, of course, be in a shape which is strong, clear, dynamic and useful.) Have the outside group look at the center shape together, observe it, point out what is strong about the shape.

Note *opposition* if and when it occurs; note Repetition if and when it occurs; note that powerful shapes often have an *out* for every *in*. (Shape, or more specifically the Shape of sculptural form, is "quite simply the art of depression and protuberance," wrote the sculptor Auguste Rodin.)

Then, break those two or three center people, return everyone one by one into the circle, and *repeat*.

EXERCISE 9: SHAPE—TAG SHAPE

Stand in a circle. One person runs in to the center of the circle and makes a shape. A second person runs in and adds to it. As the third person runs in, the first person comes out of the center. As the fourth person runs in, the second person comes out; as the fifth runs in, the third comes out, etc. There should always be a shape in the center, comprised of two bodies—no more, no less.

This exercise encourages the group to make shapes without thinking about it. The most important thing is to keep the flow and momentum going, to establish a rhythm within the group.

EXERCISE 10: SHAPE—THE JOURNEY

Soft focus. Become a vessel for Shape. Begin traveling with Shape, concentrating on the tension and constant interplay between *extension* and *contraction*: open and close, out and in. Let Shape take you on a journey. As you travel, allow others to affect your journey. Respond, in Shape, to Shape. Make choices based on other people's shapes, their patterns of expansion and contraction, and let their shapes lead you on a journey. Let them take you over, let them give you direction, guide you around the space.

EXERCISE 11: ARCHITECTURE

Gather the group in the center of the room. Ask them to look around and see the room as a stage set, to find a specific piece of architecture that inspires movement. Then ask for one volunteer to run to her/his selected *set* and perform a repeated action with (or off of) it. Ask another person to run and join. Let the two develop their movement in the given setting. Bring them back to the group. Ask for another volunteer. Repeat.

In this exercise it is important that you steer the group away from the literal and the obvious. They should be encouraged to move without knowing why, to perform action without knowing what it is.

This is a good example of Viewpoints training as the practice of *imagination* and *spontaneity*. When we know what a door is and what it can do, we limit both ourselves and the possibility of the door. When we are open to its *size* and *texture* and *shape*, a door can become anything, and everything. The gift of Viewpoints training is allowing us to see old things in news ways—to wake up the sleeping form—to experience the room as if for the first time, to find surprising and new possibility in ourselves, our environment and our art.

OBSERVATIONS

To do the "not-to-do," or, "Pay no attention to the man behind the curtain."

One of the problems that often arises in early Viewpoints training is the fact that while all the work is designed to get the participants out of their heads, you are introducing ideas and instructions that require thought. They are listening to your words, it is impossible *not* to think, it's like saying: "Do not imagine pink elephants," or, "Pay no attention to the man behind the curtain." Acknowledge this dilemma with the group. It is natural and unavoidable. You practice Viewpoints to become more conscious. But in the beginning, you will feel *self*-conscious. Later, with practice and perseverance, this self-consciousness dissolves into a kind of hyper-consciousness—a constant state of heightened awareness that is achieved without effort or thought. It simply becomes part of who you are and how you perceive the world.

The Gray Zone: "wenn schon, dann schon."

Use the early Viewpoints training to exit the Gray Zone, where things are expected, safe, comfortable, middle-of-the-road. Enter the state of mind which the Germans refer to as "wenn schon, dann schon," an expression that translates literally to: "When already, then already," but is commonly used to mean: "If then, then then," or, "If you do it, *do it*." Do it all the way. Live in the extreme. By pushing ourselves into the furthest reaches of Tempo and Distance and Shape, for instance, we become more comfortable with these extremes and are therefore more likely to call on them when needed in our work: the expressive range of the artist is widened. Once again, the training is about opening up possibility and providing you with more choice.

Eventually you will return to an area of nuance and subtlety, but by then the "gray" will be chosen and shaped by you, as opposed to it being a necessary fallback position springing from fear. For today, live in the black-and-white; be definite, clear, bold, radical.

The litmus test—Viewpoints as a mirror.

The Individual Viewpoints provide a litmus test for the individual performer: they serve as a checklist for assessing abilities and limitations. Encourage the group to pay attention to their individual leanings and avoidances, to parts of the body that are hurt or hidden, to fallback positions and unconscious patterns.

In beginning Viewpoints work, one cannot avoid seeing oneself. Individuals become hyper-aware of all sorts of things, from how much they stand outside of themselves to how delayed their reaction time is to how much they hate the length of their arms or the bounce of their walk. The mirror becomes so big and horrifying. But keep reminding the group that the way *around* is actually *through*. Self-consciousness is a kind of prison, consciousness is freedom.

Practice what you preach.

The most essential quality in teaching Viewpoints is being open to what actually occurs in the group rather than what you had hoped would occur. Viewpoints training needs practice on the part of the instructor/leader/director as well as the participants. The only times we've witnessed Viewpoints "failing" is when the instructor has had a set and rigid way of teaching, a prescribed plan for the session. Teaching Viewpoints requires extreme awareness on the part of the instructor. Remain open to the particular obstacles and dynamics that arise within your group: adjust your plan, stay on a single Viewpoint longer if necessary, skip another if it's beneficial in the present moment, watch with an eagle eye and lead the group according to what happens *in the moment*—if they take the session somewhere unexpected, go with it.

The practicing of Viewpoints by the performers and the teaching of Viewpoints by the leader demand openness. The scenario is the same as with actors entering a scene: know what you want, enter, and be prepared to adjust to what you are given. Let go of all preconceived ideas and be where you are. Listen. Receive. Respond. *Use it.*

Tina's experience.

I went to teach a three-week session at the Steppenwolf summer school. I had just closed a production (*Bells Are Ringing*), flown in on an early morning plane, and was in no mood to teach. I arrived only to discover that we had been booked into a different space than the one in which I had taught the previous summer. The new space was the Steppenwolf Garage, currently being used for a production, and the Viewpoints class was relegated to what had become a lobby of sorts: a thin sliver of space defined by black hanging velours with paintings displayed on them. I turned to the administrator and complained: "You can't do Viewpoints in here. You should know better! There's no room to move, and we'll have to watch out for the paintings, which is the antithesis of freedom and abandon! I can't work in here." He went out to see if he could find another space. In the meantime, I sat down with the students, begrudgingly introduced myself, and asked them how their first day of school was the day before. They told me that it was good except they sat around and talked too much. Between the talking yesterday and the cold in the air on this morning, they couldn't wait to get up and move. Oh no! I thought for a moment, then told them how I was about to cancel the session—and just talk—but that would be against everything I wanted to share with them about the value of Viewpoints. I told them that for me, above all else, Viewpoints is about learning to work with what you are given: obstacle as opportunity. I took a deep breath, and got us up on our feet to begin training.

I finished with this group after three weeks. In the last three weeks of their nine-week summer session, they again practiced Viewpoints but with another teacher (an actress in Chicago with whom I had worked on three productions and whom I recommended to continue the training). I returned to Chicago to watch a final class, which included "presentations" in front of an audience. The group was well into Open Viewpoints (see Chapter 6) when the teacher began adding key words, themes, directives. She had said earlier that the session was dedicated to: "flying, freedom, play." The group was in the middle of developing an amazing sequence of danger and imbalance, when she said: "The theme is *flying*." Now sometimes it is wonderful to intentionally switch gears in a radical fashion, to purposely slam into the opposite, however, in this case, it was clear that the teacher had this preconceived "theme" in mind, that it was a goal she was planning to demonstrate to the small invited audience. It had nothing to do with the experience the group was deep inside of, and as a result, they found it impossible to switch. I sat for about fifteen minutes listening to the instructor continue to call out words that would steer the group in the direction she wanted. All the time, unpredictable and profound moments were happening in front of her, yet she missed them as she continued to force the experience.

CHAPTER 6

PUTTING THE INDIVIDUAL VIEWPOINTS TOGETHER

Once a familiarity with the individual Physical Viewpoints has been achieved, it is time to put them all together. The preliminary exercises found in Chapter 4: How to Begin? ensure that everyone is able to work onstage with spontaneity and a extensive awareness of others. The exercises from Chapter 5: Introducing the Individual Viewpoints ensure an acquaintance with the individual Viewpoints and sensitivity to the overall stage picture. These exercises are for the next stage of Viewpoints training.

DEEPENING THE PRACTICE

EXERCISE 1: COUNTING

1. Begin with a counting exercise in which everyone walks in the space at a similar speed but in any direction. For exam-

ple, if there are twenty people, ask the group to attempt to count from one to twenty without more than one person ever speaking at the same time, so everyone is counting a different number out loud. Each person is to speak only once in the course of counting to twenty. Once someone has counted a number, they are not to count again. If more than one person speaks at a time the group must start the counting all over again. If they have trouble doing this, ask them to listen and focus with more attention to the whole.

2. To cultivate listening even further, have the participants continue walking with *soft focus* while heightening awareness of their tempo. Everyone should walk at the same speed. Then, once established, each person should accelerate her/his speed, again in coordination with the other group members. Then each person should break into a run together; when acceleration reaches a peak, everyone should change to a deceleration together, slowing down as a group. From a medium walking speed the entire group should attempt to stop together at the same instant. In the moment the body stops, the internal energy accelerates.

3. After several moments of stillness, the group attempts to start walking again at the same instant and at a precise and unison speed.

EXERCISE 2: THE FLOW

Once the group has worked with Tempo this way, ask them to continue walking with *soft focus* and to add a heightened awareness of space. Now the five options (1–5 in the list below) that comprise The Flow can be introduced one at a time. With each addition, the previous options should remain in play until all five are happening together. *Always, when working with Viewpoints, the choices are made intuitively and based on surrounding events.* Allow several minutes before adding any new option so that the participants can fully explore what happens with each new addition.

1. Walk through the space created between two people. Imagine that this space is a *doorway* to pass through. Continue walking in the space, passing through all of the available *doors* that appear around you. Because of the constant presence of new doors, you will find yourself moving in unexpected directions as you move around the room.

2. Change tempo. The tempo changes are inspired by the tempo changes of others and by the action of passing through doors made by the space between two people.

3. Add the possibility of stopping. As before, the stops are inspired by external events, i.e., other people stopping or going. Inside of the stillness of a stop is a great deal of energy and wakefulness.

4. Follow someone. It may happen that lines occur in space.

5. As opposed to passing through a door, you can now also turn away from someone as you come into their proximity. You can turn in the opposite direction.

6. Once all five of these options are in play, allow the group to find a natural flow. After a while you may ask them to form a diagonal line in space while keeping these five options in play. There will be a beautiful fluidity of movement and stillness as this exercise continues. Allow the group to explore the freedom inside a diagonal line for at least three or four minutes.

7. Open the exercise up again to the whole space. After a while different variations are possible within the five options. Have the group work with an awareness of different kinds of lines in space. For example, (1) form a line upstage from stage left to right. Maintaining the five options in movement, one person at a time turns to face downstage, while everyone else faces upstage. Everyone needs to be aware of who is facing downstage so that when s/he turns upstage, someone else can turn downstage. (2) Form a line upstage from stage left to right, facing downstage. Continuing the five options, slowly move together downstage to form a line on the downstage edge of the space. The exercise ends when everyone is stopped still in a line all the way downstage, facing the audience.

Note: The Flow is an instant invitation to instinctual movement and a sense of fluidity of movement in relation to other people. It is helpful to practice The Flow often. If there are enough participants, it is a good idea to occasionally divide into two groups, so that one group watches while the other practices The Flow. Watching others can clarify a great deal. Being watched by a group heightens the stakes onstage.

EXERCISE 3: LANE WORK

1. Five to seven participants stand upstage in a horizontal line, stage left to stage right, etc. They are equidistant, allowing a minimum of several feet between each other. The space in front of each person forms a lane (imagine a swimming pool). The participants face downstage; they are motionless and attentive, listening to each other. They will face the following limitations when they begin to move:
2. Each person must remain inside her/his lane. The lane extends ideally about twenty feet. Each person is free to move back and forth to any part of her/his lane. But:
3. Movement is strictly limited to five options: (1) walking, (2) running, (3) jumping, (4) dropping, (5) stillness.
4. Each maintains an awareness of the space formed by all of the lanes and stays in tune with all the other participants at every moment.
5. Each makes choices with particular attention to the following Viewpoints: Kinesthetic Response, Spatial Relationship, Repetition, Duration and Tempo. (There should be no obvious use of Architecture, Shape or Gesture in this exercise.) The Topography has already been predetermined by the lanes. While doing Lane Work, there is no time to think about the individual Viewpoints, rather the participants must use all they have learned so far *intuitively*, in the moment, and in response to what is happening already.
6. As the participants are ready and standing in their beginning positions, you may tell them to begin. An individual's

movement begins only in response to someone else's movement. To discern this movement, a high level of listening and attention must be sustained consistently. Working with *soft focus* makes direct eye contact unnecessary. The movement must occur instantaneously and with a full physical commitment. The beginning of movement in the lanes should appear organic and easy, as if there is no leader or follower. If, when the exercise begins, you notice that people all moved at once or forced the movement to begin, stop them. Have them return to their initial starting points at the ends of their lanes. Remind them to listen and let everything they do come *to* them, rather than forcing it. Sometimes this means a group might just stand still for several seconds, or even a minute, before movement occurs. This is okay. The object of this exercise is to practice listening rather than to create events onstage.

Note: During Lane Work watch out for a stop/start tendency, which generally indicates that attention is being given to the beginning of a move but disintegrating into an unfocused, indiscriminate conclusion. This propensity to respond to an impulse with commitment, but then randomly stop to wait for the next impulse, results in a jerky improvisation.

When a group new to Viewpoints training begins Lane Work, it is often difficult for them to trust the limited vocabulary. There is an inbred desire in the performer to entertain or impress, so that walking suddenly becomes hopping or skipping, for instance. Allow nothing other than the basic strict actions of walking, running, jumping and dropping. Encourage the performers to trust simplicity and a minimalism of movement. (A group of people each slowly lifting one foot in unison can be a powerful dramatic moment.)

Lane Work teaches the necessity to commit fully to an action while simultaneously being able to adjust and change based upon new events. Being fully committed yet open to change simultaneously is a physical paradox that (when mastered) leads to an unusual sensation of freedom.

Through Lane Work it also becomes apparent how much one can *see* without looking around: the body listens to the entire stage. A person downstage can *hear* an upstage person move, then move in response to it.

EXERCISE 4: GRID WORK

Now is the time to allow all the individual Viewpoints to function simultaneously within the *floor pattern* of a grid (for a full description of *floor pattern*, see the Architecture and Topography sections of the previous chapter).

1. The ideal number of participants for this exercise (at this stage) is at least five and no more than nine. As in Lane Work, everyone begins upstage in a horizontal line. Unlike Lane Work, the space between the participants at the start doesn't have to be uniform, therefore choices will have been made about Spatial Relationship and Shape. The improvisation begins with stillness and an attention to the whole stage and to all individuals.

2. Based on listening and responding with a Viewpoints vocabulary, the improvisation begins. The participants are free to move in any direction that conforms to a grid pattern (no diagonal lines, no curves). Each improvisation can last any amount of time. As participants get to know the form, allow for *at least* five minutes for an exploration of the new freedom that Grid Work allows.

Do not move unless there is a reason to move, and desire for variety is not enough of a reason.

—BERTOLT BRECHT

Brecht's thinking is fully relevant to Viewpoints training. In all the improvisations, movement should be made for a reason. The reason is not psychological, but rather formal, compositional and intuitive. Viewpoints = choices made about time and space. Every move is based upon what is *already* happening. The reason to move may be a kinesthetic response to a motion or might clarify a spatial relationship or a choice about speed in relation to a tempo already present onstage. A move may be made to conform to a floor pattern or in relation to issues about duration that arise within the group. A choice may be made in relation to the existing architecture or may be a repetition of a shape or gesture. But no move should happen arbitrarily or for a desire for variety.

EXERCISE 5: OPEN VIEWPOINTS

Now the participants are ready to try Open Viewpoints, a freeform version of Viewpoints training, where floor patterns, such as the lane or grid, are not predetermined. It is a practice where a group of anywhere from five to nine people will, by employing extraordinary listening, generosity and artfulness, find a way to begin an improvisation using fully their Viewpoints training.

1. Spatial Relationship should be the first consideration. As they walk onto the stage, participants should make articulate choices about *where* to begin based on the placement of others around them. The opening arrangement should not be too baroque (not too many odd shapes), but rather a simple, visible Spatial Composition where the entire stage picture is clear to everyone. Start with stillness.
2. From stillness the participants listen to one another and to the room. They listen with their entire bodies. There should be no hurry to make something happening (when beginning an Open Viewpoints session, patience is an ally). The quality of listening creates the conditions in which something may occur: participants attend to the listening and to one another. Then they act upon that listening with a Viewpoints vocabulary.
3. The participants should be aware of the emerging movement vocabulary happening during the first few minutes of

the improvisation, and attempt to develop this finite vocabulary, rather than creating new movement ideas. For example, if a particular gesture such as *pointing*, *waving* or *saluting* occurs, stick with those shapes rather than inventing new ones. New shapes occur almost by themselves, through an involvement with the extant vocabulary.

Ideally, Lane Work has already demonstrated the maximum effect of a minimal palate. Gertrude Stein wrote from an extremely limited lexicon. She created innumerable meanings through the juxtaposition of the same words in different ways: "The same, only different," she would say (see Chapter 15, page 186). Viewpoints training emerges very much from an aesthetic similar to Stein's. The intent is not to create an ever-increasing vocabulary; rather it is to imbue new meanings into repeated shapes.

During the Open Viewpoints session, watch the stage, and coach the participants if necessary. If there are so many different things going on that you cannot see the entire stage picture and everyone in it, ask the participants to simplify and minimize their vocabulary. The group should try to stay on the *same plate*, which means that they are working together on one event rather than many. A great deal of variation exists inside a single event, but only one event is happening. When the group is not on the *same plate*, unfocused chaos and diffusion ensues; when a group finds an event together, the results can be breathtaking. This does not necessarily mean that all participants are centralized or near each other; "one event" can occur with two or three groups across space.

Note: Ultimately the best way to learn Viewpoints is practice. Generally an Open Viewpoints improvisation should last from ten to fifteen minutes. At one point early on it is a good idea to allow for an uninterrupted experience of Open Viewpoints for twenty minutes. Afterward ask each individual who participated in the longer improvisation to give a piece of advice to the next group, advice from the heat of experience. The advice should be concise, practical and to the point. Often the participants will articulate basic concepts such as: "Pay attention," "Don't think too much," "Listen with your whole body," "Have fun," "Let go," "Trust in the others," etc. As in any kind of learning, it is best for the advice to emerge from those who just had the experience rather than from an outside instructor.

EXERCISE 6: SATS

Eugenio Barba, the Artistic Director of the Odin Teatret in Denmark, asked the question: "What do all actors around the world, despite their language and cultural differences, share in common?" He calls the answer to this question "Sats," a Norwegian word that describes the quality of energy in the moment *before* an action. The action itself, post-Sats, is particular to the culture of the performer. But the quality of energy *before* the action is what all actors around the world share. The quality of the preparation, or Sats, determines the success of the action.

Take archery, for example. The archer pulls the arrow back taut inside the tension of the bow and aims. The moment before the release of the arrow constitutes the Sats. The success of the arrow's journey is decided by the quality of the moment before the release, not the release itself.

Similarly, onstage, an actor should develop an awareness of and fluency with Sats energy. In Viewpoints, Sats is visible and palpable. If Sats energy is attended to qualitatively, the movement appears more necessary and visible. The following exercise helps familiarize oneself with the nature of Sats energy.

1. Seven to nine participants form a horizontal line upstage from left to right. Each person stands in that line with the sense of gently being pulled up through the head and down into the earth: strong legs, *soft focus*, loose arms and open heart. For now, we will call this Sats Position. Once the upstage Sats Position is established, participants may move in and out of Open Viewpoints downstage of the line, returning to Sats Position when desired.

2. It is always possible to return to the upstage line to reexperience and remember the physical state of readiness or Sats, but each participant should be either fully *onstage* in Viewpoints or fully *in Sats Position*. In returning to Sats Position, the participant does not need go back to the same place on the line.

Introducing the Sats Position allows the participants to learn to give focus to smaller groups by introducing the possibility of Viewpoint solos, duets or trios.

Note: When the energy in Sats Position is intensified and accelerated, it can be riveting to watch. Because the Sats state is so concentrated and energized, any movement into Open Viewpoints emerging from Sats will feel and seem more distilled, more necessary. The stakes are raised naturally with Sats.

Actually there is no such thing as Sats Position, because Sats is a quality of energy that is used constantly onstage before any action. But the concept is a useful one for this exercise and for developing further presence in Viewpoints training.

Exercises for Further Development

The following exercises can be introduced to develop fluency, articulation, differentiation and clarity in the Open Viewpoints.

EXERCISE 1: THE FLYING PHRASES

In two or three minutes, each participant, working alone, creates a brief movement combination or phrase, which begins on one side of the space and ends on the other. The phrase should feel like flying; it should devour space, have a clear beginning, middle and end and be something that others will be able to learn quickly (and without injuring themselves). If a participant comes from a dance background it is fine for them to use that training in devising a combination.

1. Divide the participants into groups of five.

2. Choose one person from the entire group to show her/his own combination to all the groups. All five groups are to learn the combination immediately by watching.

3. The person who invented the combination stands in the middle. The first group performs the combination in unison, moving from one side of the space to the other. Count off: "5, 6, 7, 8" or "4, 3, 2, 1" to get them going. Perhaps suggest that suddenly it is opening night at a major regional theater and this combination has been rehearsed for five weeks on a LORT (B+) salary. With this attitude they are to perform as an ensemble, with a sense of what the others are doing at each instant, and with an ending that is definite and unified. If they have trouble staying together, ask them to at least "sell" the ending. Make us believe that they are a company.

4. Once the first group has performed this satisfactorily (it may take several tries) have the second group give it a try, with the originator once again in the middle. And so on. If a group performs really well, ask them to try it at double time, then half time.

Note: The point of this exercise is not the caliber of the choreography, but rather the quality of group performance. How does the group handle the sudden crisis of performance together? They should try the best they can to stay together and perform the movement in unison, but also learn to incorporate any "mistakes" gracefully.

This exercise develops fluency with Repetition. Repetition, you learn here, is not imitation, rather it is *entering into* the quality of other people's Shape and Tempo.

EXERCISE 2: THE RELAYS

1. Divide the group into four relay teams (A, B, C, D). At the same end of the space, make a lane for each team. The first

person in the lane for each team is "1," next comes "2," and so forth.

2. Each team works in isolation from the other teams, creating its own material, in its own lane. Since each team creates at the same time, it is vital for an outside eye to keep track of where people are in space and give clear commands when each team is to move.

3. "1's, go!" is the best way to start the 1's of each group. Each 1 then runs across the space, creating one action as s/he goes. It could be a turn or a leap or a hop with a clap. 1 should execute the action as articulately as possible, because everyone on her/his team needs to see it and learn it instantly.

4. Once the four 1's have completed their action they come around to the back of their team's lane. Make sure everyone has seen what 1 has done. If not, have them do it again.

5. Then: "2's, go!" All the second people in the lane now repeat what the 1's have done. As soon as the 2's begin, send the 3's, etc., until all participants have gone, *including* the 1's again. When finished moving across the floor, the participants always go around to the back of their lane.

6. Once everyone has gone through the first action, the 2's should be at the front of their relay groups. Now the 2's will, each on their own, add to what is already there, either to the beginning or ending of the 1's move. "2's, go!" Again, make sure that everyone has seen what their 2 has added.

7. "3's, go!" and so on until the 2's have gone for the second time. Of course now the 3's are adding something new, which everyone else repeats.

8. Then the 4's add on, and so forth, until all the participants have added a move and there is enough material to challenge memory and ability. It is possible to add up to ten or twelve moves without it becoming too overwhelming.

9. Once the chain of moves is completed, have the A team form a lane upstage and, much like Flying Phrases, the team should perform their whole series of moves in unison as a performance, as if it has been rehearsed for weeks.

10. Have each team take a turn, performing its own moves in unison.

11. Next, ask all the 1's to go upstage and, using their knowledge of Spatial Relationship and Architecture, find a place to begin an improvisation together. Now there are four people onstage with four different movement combinations. *Where* one moves at any time should be based on where other people are and *when* one moves is dependent upon Kinesthetic Response or a reaction to other people's movement. Each person goes through their combination one time, without internal repetitions, but with acute attention to *where* and *when* they move, based upon the three other people onstage. Upon reaching the end of a movement cycle, each 1 should hold her/his own position until everyone is finished.

12. Next the 2's try this improvisation from a new beginning position, and so on, until all groups have performed. It is then possible to mix up the groups and have seven or nine participants in an improvisation.

This relay exercise develops an acute awareness of and fluency with Kinesthetic Response, both in actually doing the improvisation as well as watching it.

EXERCISE 3: THE OBSTACLE COURSE

1. Half of the group goes onstage while the other half observes. At an unexpected moment ask everyone onstage to hold positions. Then choose one person already onstage to be the leader and ask everyone else, without looking around, to take on the leader's shape. Because everyone is frozen and can't look around, the participants are instantly dependent upon whomever they *can* see. If there is a participant who cannot see anyone, then that person should try to feel through her/his back if need be, and make a choice about Shape based on intuition and feeling.

2. The leader on the stage then begins to move through space, conscious of the others following. Everyone else tries to move at exactly the same time and in the same shape and tempo as the leader. It is vital that the group doesn't look like they are following the leader; rather, it should appear to those watching that they are performing the same actions at the exact same moment, in unison with full presence and sense of ensemble. No one should be looking furtively around toward the leader.

3. Pay particular attention to the stops. When the leader stops, everyone stops in the same instant, no matter where they are onstage. The stops should be clear and precise and dramatic.

4. After the group has found a sense of ensemble and performance quality together, change the leader. This new leader should introduce new tempos, shapes and qualities of movement. At any time it is possible to choose a new leader.

    Make sure the group that watched gets a chance to do this exercise, while the other group watches and gets a chance to learn from observation.

This exercise demands an attitude from the group that every moment is an *opening night performance* for an audience. The *follow the leader* structure should be invisible to those watching; it is merely the secret cause that motivates the action. To the audience, the event should exude performance energy and grace.

This exercise also develops an awareness of *stops* and their impact on the audience. If the stops are vague and blurry, the audience will miss their potential drama. If the stops are precise and exact, they create an exciting physical event onstage.

EXERCISE 4: FLOCKING

Half of the group spreads out onstage, facing downstage, while the other half observes. Much like the Obstacle Course (Exercise 3), the group will be doing in unison what a leader initiates. This time, though, the leader is the person who, at any given moment, cannot see anyone else. Since the exercise starts with the participants facing downstage, the leader will be the person farthest downstage, unable to see anyone else. The leader initiates moves and the others repeat the leader's shapes and movements in unison. If the leader turns during a move and is able to see someone else, s/he drops her/his role as leader. The person who cannot see anyone else becomes the new leader. The exercise goes on as new leaders continue to take over.

Bad Habits and Fallback Positions

We have noticed that certain fallback positions occur with individuals as they begin to learn Viewpoints. Here are some proclivities to watch out for (and point out to the group) as they arise. All of these weak habits occur as a substitute for trust in what is actually happening.

- Hunching over, arms extended, in a ready-for-anything pose.
- Grabbing another participant and pulling or pushing her/him where you want her/him to go. (This shows that you are trying to *make something happen* rather than trusting that *something is happening* already.)
- Forcing a predictably rhythmic pattern while stamping one's feet or clapping.
- Collapsing onto the floor and hugging the ground in vague spaghetti/pretzel shapes.
- Going in and out of *soft focus*, checking to see if you are doing the right or wrong thing.
- Limiting your kinesthetic response to falling on the ground.
- Indicating participation rather than actually getting involved. (This often manifests itself in walking like an automaton stick figure.)
- The whole group standing around in a quasi-circle, losing all awareness of Spatial Relationship, and stomping the

floor or clapping hands in tribal unison. (This is a natural, and perhaps necessary, pattern of early Viewpoints work. You will notice that after a group has worked together for a bit, it will achieve a greater subtlety, and the need for this primal group moment will be exorcised.)

□ Everyone is working in the center of the space, unable to free themselves from the ingrained notion that there is only one powerful spot onstage—dead center.

□ While the group is engaged in an event or activity, out of nowhere a person suddenly runs to the closet, pulls out a broom and acts with it because they have a "new idea."

Emotion

The gift of Viewpoints is that it leads you to, not away from, emotion. People often misunderstand the goal as being a state of neutrality and deadness as opposed to a state of aliveness, receptivity and experience. What's important to remember about Viewpoints is that, just like other "methods" of acting, the goal is to be alive and engaged onstage. The beauty of Viewpoints is that it allows us to reach this goal, not by forcing it out of ourselves, but by receiving it from others, and ourselves.

CHAPTER 7

GROUP IMPROVISATIONS

Although it is a good idea to practice Open Viewpoints daily, supplementary exercises will increase any group's ability, agility and sensitivity to issues of creating dramatic events with time and space.

SUPPLEMENTARY EXERCISES

Improvisation Exercises

The following group improvisations will augment range and expertise in Viewpoints training.

IMPROVISATION 1: THREE UP/TWO DOWN

1. Five participants go onstage. At the moment the improvisation begins, only three people should be up (standing) and

two should be down (close to the ground). As the group continues moving, they need to adhere to the rule that, at every moment, three people must be up and two down. Visible and articulate choices by the participants will help to create a clear flow of action. At any moment anyone who is down can rise up and anyone who is up can sink or drop down. The principles of Viewpoints can still be in play, but the primary focus should be on how many people are up and down.

2. After everyone has tried Three Up/Two Down, experiment with seven people doing Four Up/Three Down. Of course this exercise is much more difficult but the same issues apply. If this is successful, move on to nine people doing Five Up/Four Down, then eleven with Six Up/Five Down.

A proficiency in the Three Up/Two Down exercise will produce a marked difference in Open Viewpoints practice. The exercise augments an awareness of vertical space and a new sense of responsibility for levels in any improvisation.

It will be clear that levels are a problem in Open Viewpoints if you notice that everyone is down or everyone is up at the same time without a sense of balance.

IMPROVISATION 2: ENTRANCES AND EXITS

For this improvisation it is necessary to designate an area for exits and entrances. If you are working on a proscenium stage, make use of the wings. If the room you are working in has a door or an offstage area, allow the participants of the improvisation to leave and then return to the room. Entrances and Exits allows the participants to leave the view of the rest of the group ("the audience") at any moment of the improvisation and return at the appropriate instant.

1. Participants should start offstage (or out of the room). If there are wings or multiple doors, have the group break up into different places offstage. This improvisation begins, as

with every Viewpoints exercise, with listening. Obviously, the ability to listen to one another is immediately heightened simply by the fact that it is now more difficult. The question hangs in the air: How does this begin? When does it begin? The ground rules are the same as with any Open Viewpoints exercise, except that at this starting point one or more of the group might not be visible because of their offstage position.

2. The participants begin an Open Viewpoints session but, for the first time, incorporate entrances and exits from the visible playing space. There are no rules about when or how participants enter and exit, other than that they should be aware of and use all the Viewpoints.

This improvisation opens up many new possibilities in Viewpoints. Remarkable moments can occur when one person is left alone onstage. Or when the stage is empty. Or when all the participants enter in a line, maintaining a sustained gesture. An entrance or exit always offers an opportunity for something miraculous, the sense that anything can happen. An entrance or exit can engender great feelings of loss or it can be riotously humorous. So much is provoked by appearing and disappearing.

A Russian director once said that he could explain Stanislavsky's approach to acting with two sentences: (1) "Do not turn around unless someone calls your name"; (2) "If you come onstage, you must have a highly compelling reason; if you stay for more than an instant, you must have a monumental reason."

Every exit is an entrance somewhere else.

—TOM STOPPARD

IMPROVISATION 3: SHOES

1. Four shoes define the parameters of the space within which an Open Viewpoints session takes place. Start with the shoes placed quite close together, forming, for example, a

small square. Five people begin to improvise within this
space, which can be as small as four feet by four feet.

2. As the improvisation continues, move the shoes to change
the size and parameters of the space. For example, you can
create a long narrow space from left to right or a corridor
from upstage to downstage.

A group improvisation within a tightly confined
space makes each movement more momentous and visible.
Immediately Spatial Relationship is a larger issue, and every
move radically alters the Composition within the arena. As
the individual Viewpoints come into play, each one is
heightened by the obstacles of confinement that a defined
space creates.

3. Finally place the shoes as far away as the room allows.

The Shoes exercise heightens the sense of boundaries, limitations
and the shape of given architecture. It encourages the participants to be aware of, and responsible for, the entire stage rather
than only the space they occupy. This exercise develops an
increased awareness of the entire available space, illustrating for
the participants that the luxury of a large and expansive space
should not be taken for granted.

One day Anne was teaching a Viewpoints class, and attempted
to make a point about each actor taking personal responsibility for
the entire stage. Finally one of her students made a comparison to
Magic Johnson. He said that what made Magic Johnson a great basketball player was not just his ability to shoot from a particular area,
but his ability to make use of every inch of the court. The same is
true for an actor—you need to own every inch of the stage.

IMPROVISATION 4: CIRCLE, CLUMP, LINE

1. Ask eight people to go onstage and quickly form a circle.
Once the circle is apparent, ask them to make a clump.
Then a line. Again, a different kind of circle, another clump,
yet another kind of line, and so on.

2. After several minutes, or when the group seems familiar with the repetition of these patterns, ask them to move freely from one of these three possibilities to another in any order without being instructed. The only caveat is that all eight participants should be working toward the same formation at the same time. How they get from one formation to the next is the point of improvisation.

3. Allow the group to find as many permutations of circles, lines and clumps as possible. Notice how relationships and events seem to unfold naturally and effortlessly.

Note: The central issue in all Viewpoints improvisations is the search for consent. Without speaking, the group finds a way to playfully and artfully solve the task.

IMPROVISATION 5: CHANGING PLACE IN SPACE

1. One person at a time finds a place onstage until there are five participants in a clear Composition in Space. Their decisions about where to go and what shapes to contribute are based on where the other people are, what they are doing and the architecture at hand. Once all five are in place, ask each person onstage to look around and memorize the shapes and places.

2. Then ask them to switch places several times until each has become familiar with the other four shapes and stations. Then allow an improvisation to occur where they get from one of the five stations to the other in an open and playful way, with a sense of Kinesthetic Response, Repetition, Tempo, etc.

3. Try the same improvisation now with seven people, then nine, and so on.

This variation on Viewpoints trains participants to discern exactly where the other people onstage are at every moment, and how to incorporate this information into the improvisation.

IMPROVISATION 6: REPETITION

1. Begin an Open Viewpoints improvisation with five participants.
2. After about ten seconds of movement, stop the participants and ask them to go back to the beginning and repeat exactly what they have just done, handling time and space in precisely the same manner.
3. Allow them to repeat that first ten seconds of material, and then connect another ten or fifteen seconds of new improvisation to the end.
4. Stop once again. Go back to the beginning. Repeat the set material followed by another sequence of new open improvisation.
5. Stop again. Repeat the sequence again, adding more material. Continue the process.
6. Try this exercise with seven or nine participants. The same issues apply: learning how to coordinate an exact repetition of improvisatory material with other participants onstage.

An aspect of Viewpoints training is learning to mentally store away every event that happens onstage, with an ability to bring it all back into the vocabulary of an improvisation. This Repetition exercise helps develop this skill.

IMPROVISATION 7: BEGINNING, MIDDLE, END

1. A group of any number of people goes onstage to begin an Open Viewpoints session. Those not in the group watch the others. Anyone watching may, at a moment that feels appropriate, call out: "End!" which will terminate the improvisation.
2. A new group starts an improvisation until an onlooker shouts: "End!"

Note: Because the duration of the improvisation is controlled from outside the group, the onstage stakes are higher and each beginning, middle and end are more visible and meaningful. The onlooker learns to identify what constitutes an ending (see *jo-ha-kyu*, which is discussed in detail in Chapter 11), and the actors onstage learn a heightened responsibility for time management.

Auxiliary Exercises

AUXILIARY EXERCISE 1: PARTNERING INTO WEIGHT ACROSS THE FLOOR

1. Any number of people can perform this exercise simultaneously, but it is helpful to have at least sixteen participants. Instruct everyone to walk around the space with *soft focus*.
2. Rather than passing through the spaces between people, the participants walk toward someone until couples are formed. Without speaking, each couple makes a decision: one gives weight and the other receives her/his weight. Begin by giving or receiving exactly ten percent of the weight of the body. Even if it is not clear how much ten percent is, try to work with exactitude, as if you knew exactly how much ten percent of a person's weight would be. It is also possible that two or more receive the weight of one person. (As always, do not work in a way that causes pain or injury!)
3. Once you have given or received ten-percent weight, allow inertia to help you separate and continue moving through the space. Again, do not avoid contact. Soon you will find yourself with someone new, and again the silent decision is made about who gives weight and who receives.
4. With each new partner, find a new solution about how to give or receive the weight. Use new parts of the body and find ways to partner that are different from habitual or polite methods.
5. Now raise the percentage of weight taken to twenty-five, leaving seventy-five percent of the weight on the floor. This

demands more exactitude and new solutions for how to partner with someone. As the percentage rises in the exercise, it will become more evident that two or three or more can support one person's weight. Again, without speaking, make sure that new solutions are found with each new partner.

6. After a while, raise the percentage to fifty: half of a person's body weight remains on the floor. Do not strain; search for fluidity and use inertia in moving from situation to situation.

7. Next try seventy-five percent.

8. Now try ninety percent. This one is quite difficult, because exactly ten percent of the person's body weight must remain on the floor.

9. Finally give or lift one hundred percent of the weight off the floor.

    Find new solutions for each person. Let the partnering be in twos, threes, fours or larger groups. Keep it moving. Finally carry the weight across the floor, finding a new solution for each encounter.

10. Now divide into two groups: one half on one side of the space in a line facing the other half on the opposite side, also in a line. Ask each person to choose eight specific people on the other side of the room (or a lesser number, if there are fewer than sixteen people), and study them, memorizing how they look and what they are wearing, etc. With closed eyes try to remember all eight and the details of how they look.

11. After the eight are memorized, open the eyes and have the entire group begin to sing "aaah" in unison (take a few moments to practice singing while still standing at opposite sides of the room, since this will be crucial to the exercise later). Anyone can change pitch at any time but the group should attempt to maintain harmonic integrity. Everyone will be responsible for the entire conglomeration of pitches so that the communal sound is full, resonant and melodious.

12. Once the group has begun to sing together, give the signal to one side to start crossing to the other side, each person walking to one of the eight people s/he has memorized.

Then each individual, still singing, lifts and carries one of her/his eight people across the entire space, completely from one side to the other, each time finding a different method of carrying. Once the exercise has begun anyone can lift at any time or from any side of the room, but no one may lift a person from the middle of the space. The carrier is responsible for her/his partner's weight and safety. If a smaller person is having trouble carrying a larger person, help can be offered, but the helper may not count this as one of her/his eight to be carried. (Be sure to remind everyone not to carry in such a way that pain or injury result. And this is not a race; there should be no hurry.)

13. This action continues until each participant has carried their designated eight people across the space, all the while singing, until everyone has finished carrying. Then, all together, the group should find a glorious finish to the singing and to the exercise.

    Because the exercise is quite strenuous, remind the participants that as they get fatigued, their tendency will be to forget to sing, and the integrity of the communal sound will be lost. In those moments, ask them to try to keep the sound open and full and in harmony with the other voices.

Note: This partnering exercise develops a sense of how limited the choices tend to be when direct physical contact is involved. The participants must search, nonverbally, to find new ways to encounter one another.

AUXILIARY EXERCISE 2: FEEDBACK EXERCISE

1. Divide into groups of three. Designate who in each group is number 1, 2 and 3. Ask each 1 what it is they crave, what sensations they yearn for, what they need. For five minutes, 1 can ask 2 and 3 to do whatever it is that would satisfy those needs. (They can ask for anything as long as it doesn't involve leaving the room.) It might be a back massage, it might be

that they want to be lifted high, or sung to or praised. The 1's should not only ask for what they want, but also concentrate on receiving it openly. They should be sensitive to the moment that the desire is fulfilled or is changed, and alter their requests accordingly. The 1's are the only participants allowed to speak unless they specifically ask the 2's and 3's of their group to speak.

2. After five minutes, without discussion, switch: now the 2's of each group ask for what they want from the 1's and 3's.

3. After five minutes, the 3's have their turn.

4. After all three participants in each group have enjoyed their five minutes of desire-fulfillment, ask 1 of each group to close her/his eyes. It is now up to 2 and 3 of each group to take the sight-deprived 1 on a five-minute journey. They should attempt to guide 1 with contact other than their hands. This journey also must stay within the room, but should include certain sensations 1 must experience: at some point during the five-minute sequence, 1 should feel as though s/he is flying; at some point 1 should be able to run freely without fear and without being touched; when the five minutes are up and the 1's are asked to open their eyes, they should be surprised at where they are.

5. Without discussion, switch to the 2's, who close their eyes and are given a journey by the 1's and 3's for five minutes.

6. Finally the 3's are given a journey by the 1's and 2's.

7. Afterward, have the entire group squat down, heads tipped forward, heels on the ground, in a circle. Ask them all to close their eyes and try to relive the journeys they just had. They should be free to vocalize responses as they remember the sensations. Ask individuals to describe an experience they had while on their journeys. They might mention words like "disorientation" or "flying" or "trust" or "thrill" or "adventure." Point out that these are the keys to *feedback*.

Note: This exercise introduces the role of *feedback* in Viewpoints training. We previously discussed the importance of balancing *feedforward* and *feedback* (see Chapter 4, page 34). Not only is each participant responsible for the *feedforward*—the outgoing energy, generosity and responsiveness toward the group, the audience and the arc of the event—but each must also allow herself/himself to receive and viscerally experience the resulting sensations that are triggered by the action. This reception is called *feedback*. And *feedback* cannot be faked or indicated. It is actual.

For example, when we think of the actor Alan Cumming, who performed the role of Master of Ceremonies in *Cabaret* on Broadway, we mostly remember the contagious pleasure of his performance. We go to the theater not only to follow a through-line, but also to empathize with an actor's thrill and experience of the fiction. As an audience, we hook our wagons to an actor's experience: the actor is like an astronaut, out in space for us, taking in the universe.

In this *feedback* exercise, the entire point is to open up the senses to allow for the sensations of the event, in order to experience the journey provided. The work is not just about being in the correct spatial relationship or moving at the right tempo; it is also about the actual, visceral experience that Viewpoints provokes. And ultimately, an actor must be able to share this experience in public.

FOUR VARIETIES OF ENERGY

There are four specific varieties of energy available to every actor at each and every moment.

1. HORIZONTAL ENERGY. Connects actors with one another and with the world around them. The tendency when first beginning Viewpoints training is to lean too heavily on horizontal energy.
2. VERTICAL ENERGY. Connects an actor to nature and the universe. Like a tree, the actor becomes the line that unites heaven and earth. This energy reaches down into the ground and up into the sky and unites the actor with the immensity of the universe.

3. HEAVY ENERGY. Is young, rambunctious, visible, unrefined energy. It throws itself against walls and seems to never run out of vitality. When first beginning Viewpoints training, heavy energy is the most accessible.

4. LIGHT ENERGY. Is more difficult to cultivate; it is mature and subtle. Less is visible on the exterior while more is going on in the interior.

It is possible to adjust and alternate these energies in the body purposefully and artfully. For example, two actors playing an intense scene close together, tend toward too much horizontal energy and not enough vertical. They lean in toward one another, and sometimes even cancel out the audience. In a moment of close proximity, try to intensify the vertical energy in contrast to the natural inclination to be extra-horizontal. This involves an increased awareness of your relationship to vertical space and will result in an adjustment that is first internal but usually also causes a visible, external shift. Similarly, in playing scenes of isolation, the tendency is for too much vertical energy. Try, in that moment, to intensify the horizontal.

RELATIONSHIP

In our exploration of the theater as both a horizontal and vertical arena, it is also interesting to ask: "I play *to* whom?" "I act *for* whom?" Throughout the history of (Western) world drama, the actors' primary relationship onstage has shifted several times. We can identify five basic types of Relationship:

1. TO THE GODS. In the Ancient Greek and Roman amphitheaters, actors spoke directly to stone statues of the gods, placed high above and behind the audiences. Each spectator was literally caught in the midst of this dramatic relationship between the human and the divine.

2. TO THE ROYALTY. During the Renaissance and the heyday of court theaters, actors played directly to and for the centrally

placed royalty, who usually sat in the first balcony, not as high up as *the gods*, but still above the masses.

3. TO THE AUDIENCE. By the nineteenth century, actors were encouraged most often to play directly out front: to and for the general audience, culminating in such forms of popular entertainment as melodrama and vaudeville.

4. TO OTHER ACTORS. With the advent of naturalism and such playwrights as Ibsen and Chekhov, actors began to face one another. The "fourth wall" was born, and continues to dominate our theater today.

5. TO NOTHINGNESS. Along comes Samuel Beckett and the actors' relationship is with the void, the emptiness. The focus of Relationship has shifted from the cosmic, to the human, to the existential. It is a bleak and distinct relationship.

In the spirit of postmodernism, we consider ourselves free to pick and choose whatever relationship we deem useful from the full history of the theater. The theater of the twenty-first century ranges freely, and often within one piece, among these various types of relationships.

CHAPTER 8

WORKING WITH MUSIC

The introduction of music suggests new possibilities in View-points training and should occur after the individual View-points have been taught and put together. Music is a vastly powerful and seductive element in the theater and to introduce it before the individual Viewpoints have been digested would be, in a sense, too great a temptation, too strong a stimulus. Introduced at the right moment, music becomes a portal: an inspiration, a boost and a challenge.

When you introduce music, it is like bringing another actor onstage. The individual or group must now deal with another *artist's* sense of time, and they'll need to adjust to it and incorporate it. Music is a partner. And also a great gift, because, like Viewpoints training itself, music leads to an expansion of possibility.

NUTS AND BOLTS IN PREPARATION

There are two ways to work with music in your sessions: one is live, the other prerecorded. In either case, there is a human being who is controlling the music, who is, in a way, *Viewpointing* with the group, determining selection, duration of each piece, volume, etc. It is crucial that the individual(s) watch, listen and respond to what is actually going on in the room. Like a good deejay, the instructor is there to inspire, to charge, to keep the fire lit. Sometimes this will mean picking up the tempo, other times it will mean letting the group work in silence.

For the following exercises, you should assume the music is prerecorded, played on a sound system and controlled by the teacher, director or sound person. You can use a console, a boom box, etc., but it is crucial that the system used produces enough sound so that the entire group can hear the music well from any point in the space. A tinny boom box would not work well in spaces such as a gym or ballroom. It is preferable to work with a system that enables quick shifts from one piece of music to another without having to stop and start, or to use two independent systems, such as two boom boxes, or one cassette player and one CD player, etc. In this fashion, you can switch from one piece of music to another, then reset something new in the first player while the second is on.

If you only have one source of music, it becomes necessary to vary how you get in and out of music so that the pattern of silence and music does not become predictable. In one case you might fade the music out slowly, in another stop it suddenly; you might hold the silence for short or long periods of time, and then bring in music suddenly and loudly, or fade in the music almost imperceptibly.

The first thing you'll notice when putting on a piece of music during Viewpoints training is that the group immediately moves to it, and the openness and unpredictability of the work are compromised. The group begins to dance *to* the music: They are imprisoned rather than freed.

There are many aspects of music that can easily *dictate* movement rather than *motivate* or suggest it:

1. TEMPO. Put on a piece of music that is slow and people will move slowly, put on a piece that is fast and they will move quickly. The same holds true for:
2. RHYTHM. Put on a waltz and people will emphasize the 1 or downbeat of every three beats.
3. HARMONY. Put on a harmonic chorale and the group will make round, lovely images, put on dissonance and the work will be jagged or violent.
4. DYNAMIC OR VOLUME. Put on something quiet and the group will work small, put on something loud and they will work large. It never fails . . . at first.

These *cause and effect* relationships between music and movement are natural. Both are organic, springing from intuition and inborn body rhythms, and also deeply associative, springing from a vast and (probably) semiconscious reservoir of cultural images. We are bound by both these instincts and these associations which have probably hardened over the years into *habits* of which we are not even aware. Working with music in Viewpoints training is yet another way to increase awareness of these patterns, and thereby increase one's ability to choose, thereby expanding one's range.

There is nothing wrong in being a slave to the music when it is first introduced *as long as it is noted*. Our ultimate goal when working with music is not to be held captive by it but rather to use it as a springboard, to let it open up, rather than shut down, possibilities. The first step toward this expansion is often a necessary awareness of limitation. It is sometimes unavoidable in the case of this most powerful of tools.

EXERCISE 1: "TO" AND "AGAINST"

The group begins to walk around the space. Put on a piece of music and instruct the group to let the music inform the walk. Choose a piece of music that is definitive in its rhythm and tempo: a march, a techno beat, a hymn. The group will inevitably begin walking *to* the music, and in some cases might even lean toward illustrating it, *acting out* their idea of it. (They might even start including Shape and Gesture.) Ask them to note this, and then to move *against* the tempo and/or rhythm, to move in *counterpoint*. If necessary, remind them that they can only walk, nothing more exists in their current vocabulary; they can walk fast or slow or in hyper-speed, etc., but they can only walk. Explore at least five or six different tempos of walking in relationship to one piece of music which is constant in its tempo. In this way, very simply, we practice freeing ourselves from being slaves to the music.

EXERCISE 2: STARTING WITH MUSIC

An alternate way for introducing music is to begin a session with music as the group warms up. The warm-up could be anything from sun salutations (as described in Chapter 4, Exercise 2) to general, informal stretching. After the warm-up, have the group begin to move around the space. Simply let the music continue to play. For this exercise it is best to use a gentle and fairly constant piece, maybe a classical adagio or an atmospheric New Age instrumental. Add an awareness of Spatial Relationship. Then add Kinesthetic Response. Then Tempo, Duration and Repetition. The group will naturally find themselves working within the texture of the music, but with a shifting variety of tempos.

Note: If the group is doing exactly what the music is dictating, turn the music off. The group is, in effect, busted. They will know they were caught not fully awake. Give them time to return to simply moving through the space in silence (with awareness of Tempo, Duration, Kinesthetic Response, Spatial Relationship and Topography), then add a new piece of music.

The ultimate goal is neither to work exclusively *to* or *against*, but *with*, in concert with. As the music work continues, think of music as a scene partner, as another member of the group. Its task is to affect and move you. Your task is to be open to it. Think of it as you would the architecture, that it is there to play *with*, dance *with*, to embrace in one moment, ignore in the next. You can illustrate the music, yes, certainly, but you can also fight it, comment on it, flirt with it, hail it.

The ultimate goal is to create the impression, both for the performers and the audience, that the music is coming from the actors' bodies—it should be *that* organic and integrated.

EXERCISE 3: OPEN VIEWPOINTS WITHOUT RHYTHM

Choose a piece of music that is relatively abstract or atmospheric, something with a lot of texture and not a lot of rhythm (for example, ambient or New Age). Do Open Viewpoints with the piece of music. The group will get used to hearing music without it manipulating them, simply because you are working with sound that is present but not domineering in its rhythm.

EXERCISE 4: OPEN VIEWPOINTS WITH RHYTHM

Choose a piece of music similar to that used in Exercise 1: a strong, repetitive beat. Do Open Viewpoints with this piece of music. Encourage the group's awareness of Tempo, Duration and Kinesthetic Response, so that they do not get stuck in the music and lose touch with Viewpoints. Encourage them to work with as much surprise and variety as they discovered in the previous exercise, when the music was less obviously binding.

EXERCISE 5: MUSIC AS THEME

Choose a smaller group to work in the space, ideally three to six individuals. Have them find a starting point: an opening position that is strong Spatially and Architecturally. Have them begin Open Viewpoints, but fairly immediately after they start, begin a piece of music. Tell them to use the music as *theme*, as *inspiration*. They should let it inform and create the world of their piece. Let the music lead them to specificity of Gesture, to a particular use of Architecture. This is the equivalent of dropping in a theme to Open Viewpoints (see Chapter 13, especially Compositions Toward a Play and the theme/Composition exercises within that section). You should choose a piece of music that is extremely evocative and specific: calliope to suggest childhood or circus, military march to suggest drills or war, spaghetti-western music, Charleston, '60s drug-trip guitar or sitar, etc.

EXERCISE 6: MUSIC AS COUNTERPOINT

A small group (three to six individuals) works in Open Viewpoints. Their task is to work in *opposition* to the music: if the music is soothing they should work aggressively, if it is fast they should work slowly, etc. Switch music often.

The Ability to Juggle. In these exercises it's crucial that individuals be able to maintain their awareness of the group and that they do not begin working as soloists with the music. The goal is to balance the impact of Open Viewpoints with that of the music. If the music takes over, turn it off immediately and, while the group continues working, remind them to work off each other. Repeat the phrases: "Stick with the Viewpoints." "Listen to each other." "Put your focus on others."

As we discussed in Chapter 5, incorporating the individual Viewpoints is like learning to juggle. At first, one might be able to have only two balls in the air. You practice and achieve three, then four, and so on. Music is another ball in the air. Text will be yet another (see next chapter). It takes practice to *add* music without dropping one of the other balls. Music should never exist at the expense of an individual Viewpoint: it should be added when the group can juggle enough balls simultaneously (and with enough ease) so that a brand-new element will not decrease awareness of Viewpoints. You'll probably drop a ball or two. That's okay. Pick up the balls, start again, find your rhythm, add the music.

EXERCISE 7: RAISING THE STAKES

Start Open Viewpoints with ambient music playing. Then change to something with a tiny bit more event in it: shifts, stops, bursts. As the group gets used to the music, treating it like another actor in the space, start raising the stakes through your musical choices: (1) switch to increasingly dramatic pieces of music; (2) change the music at more unexpected intervals; (3) slam from one style into its opposite; (4) play two pieces of music at once, work in the extremes, inviting the group to as well.

EXERCISE 8: THE SOUNDS OF SILENCE

After you've worked a while with music, go back to the *silence* of the room for Open Viewpoints. Point out how *silence* is actually full of sounds which might not at first be audible or deemed useful. Work off these sounds. Think of these sounds as the *music* with which you are now *Viewpointing*. Listen—work off bodies shifting, a creak in the floor, a car horn from outside, a siren, etc.

Auxiliary Exercises for Working with Music

AUXILIARY EXERCISE 1

Incorporate musical selections that have spoken text in them; encourage the group to work off the text as well as the music. If you do this exercise after speaking has been introduced, encourage the group to speak and move off the recording, to echo it, answer it, twist it.

AUXILIARY EXERCISE 2

Choose a piece of thematically specific music or clearly delineated genre music. Give the group a setting or character types or both.

And begin Open Viewpoints. For example, have the group work against a wall or with a specific door or in a corner. Then give them the setting of an alleyway or a bar or a street at night. Then state the theme of, e.g., film noir, and play a piece of cool '50s jazz or something from a noir film.

THINGS WE'VE LEARNED IN WORKING WITH MUSIC

- ◻ In listening to music, you can learn both from the composition and from the performance. The way Glenn Gould plays Bach is remarkably different from the way Keith Jarrett does. Same musical notes—a world of difference.

- ◻ Music can deaden. We recently observed a Viewpoints session in which the instructor put on a piece of music (a contemporary pop tune she loved) and let it play for three or four minutes. It became the equivalent of the group sticking with an activity or tempo without possibility for change. Lack of change put the group to sleep. They were *Viewpointing* all right, but were on automatic pilot. The reliability of the music put the performers to sleep. When serving as *deejay* during Viewpoints training, the most essential awareness to develop is that of Duration. How long, how short, do you leave on a piece of music? When do you change, and in response to what? Again, Duration is about knowing how long to stay in something (in this case a piece of music), so that something occurs, so that you exploit the moment of actual event, but not so long that it starts to fall asleep or die.

- ◻ Well-known or current pop tunes are not great to work with, except as an aerobic warm-up or in very short installments. Songs that the group knows (and will want to sing along with or dance to) are usually the most limiting.

- ◻ Different kinds of music work best for different levels of Viewpoints training. In general, graduate from the least intrusive to the most.

Music for Beginning Viewpoints

Use pieces without lyrics, which are atmospheric, ambient, repetitive, open:

> Will Ackerman
> Cirque du Soleil
> Philip Glass
> Henryk Górecki
> Gregorian chant
> John Hodian
> Wim Mertens
> Michael Nyman
> Penguin Cafe Orchestra
> Rachel's
> Steve Reich
> Adagios (see Samuel Barber's "Adagio for Strings," Gustav Mahler's Fourth Symphony, Maurice Ravel's "Pavane for a Dead Princess")

Music for Middle Viewpoints

Introduce pieces that evoke time, place, image, genre:

> Johann Sebastian Bach
> Carla Bley
> John Lurie
> Wolfgang Amadeus Mozart
> Arvo Pärt
> Astor Piazzolla
> Tom Verlaine
> Tom Waits
> Big Band/Swing (Cab Calloway, Tommy Dorsey, Glenn Miller)
> Country (Johnny Cash, Patsy Cline, Hank Williams)

Music for Advanced Viewpoints

Add music which is erratic, unpredictable, extreme, attention-getting:

Ludwig van Beethoven

Heiner Goebbels

György Ligeti

Gustav Mahler

Einstürzende Neubauten

Arnold Schoenberg

Igor Stravinsky

Anton Webern

John Zorn

CHAPTER 9

STARTING TO SPEAK

As elements accumulate in the process of Viewpoints training, there comes the moment for the human voice. Vocal Viewpoints addresses sound in the same way that the Physical Viewpoints addresses movement, i.e., by increasing an awareness of pure sound separate from psychological or linguistic meaning. Rather than hearing only what a certain word connotes, we start to address how it sounds and how the sound itself contains information and expressivity. Additionally, habit and fear too often engender a narrow range in an actor's physical and vocal exploration. Vocal Viewpoints highlights the limitations of one's vocal range and subsequently encourages more radical and dynamic vocal choices.

Vocal Viewpoints generates an adventurous attitude to the voice's potential through freedom, control and responsiveness. As an actor-training tool, the introduction of these *points of view* can be invaluable in cultivating vocal virtuosity. During the rehearsal of a play, the time set aside for Vocal Viewpoints training offers a chance to deal with the play's text nonpsychologically, which, in turn, opens up rich new possibilities within scene work. Changing vocality can alter meaning and impact.

The Vocal Viewpoints are slightly different than the Physical Viewpoints (for instance, we do not work with Topography). When working on the Vocal Viewpoints, we use: Tempo, Duration, Repetition, Kinesthetic Response, Shape, Gesture, Architecture, Pitch, Dynamic, Acceleration/Deceleration, Timbre and Silence. These Viewpoints should be introduced one at a time. Developing with each individually will lead to a remarkable awareness of the potential of the vocal instrument, for both the speaker and the listener.

INTRODUCING THE INDIVIDUAL VOCAL VIEWPOINTS

Starting Solo

Each participant works alone at first, choosing a place in the room where s/he can most effectively concentrate on her/his own voice and sound. Ask each person to make up a three-syllable word of gibberish, e.g., "ka-bing-zong," "yip-eed-oh," etc.

EXERCISE 1: PITCH

1. Start at your lowest possible pitch, intoning your three-syllable gibberish word, and continue repeating it, with each repetition rising a notch in pitch. The exercise is complete when you are vocalizing your word at the highest possible (and safe) pitch in your range.
2. Work individually, experimenting with switching pitch on each syllable of your word. For instance, try low/low/high *or* very high/very high/medium low, etc. Try creating as many combinations as possible.

Note: This exercise heightens awareness of our traditionally limited pitch range, and strengthens ability to expand that range.
The same holds true for the exercises that follow in terms of
expanding the performers' dynamic range, temporal range, etc.

EXERCISE 2: DYNAMIC

1. Starting at your most quiet volume (barely audible), speak
   your gibberish word, and continue repeating it, with each
   repetition increasing a notch in volume. The exercise is
   complete when you are vocalizing your word at the loudest
   (but still safe) possible volume.
2. Now experiment with switching dynamic, or volume, on
   each syllable of the word, e.g., loud/barely audible/medium
   or quiet/loud/quiet, etc.

EXERCISE 3: TEMPO AND DURATION

Repeat the same form as above except in terms of Tempo, moving
from the slowest possible speed to the fastest. Then switch tempo/
duration on each syllable.

EXERCISE 4: TIMBRE

Experiment with your gibberish word using different physical
resonators to produce the sound, e.g., nasal, from your abdomen,
your throat, etc. Mix and match as above.

EXERCISE 5: SHAPE

1. Ask the participants to take their three-syllable gibberish
   word and, still working individually, adjust the vowels and
   consonants as necessary to produce a word which is made

of *round* shapes. What sounds feel *round*? Why? Which are clearly not? Now change the syllables into a gibberish word which is *linear* or *jagged* in its component shapes.

2. Mix and match as above.

3. Think of and say aloud to yourself recognizable words from the English language (or any other language) which are specifically *round, soft* or *fluid* in shape, or specifically *sharp, spiky* or *percussive*.

EXERCISE 6: GESTURE

Just as in Physical Viewpoints, Vocal Viewpoints can be either Expressive or Behavioral. We learn to make *Vocal Gestures*, which are sounds with a beginning, middle and end, unlike words which have specific linguistic definitions.

Expressive. Each individual produces a series of Expressive Vocal Gestures on their own. These are sounds that are not of everyday behavior but, rather, express in a more abstract way a state of being, an emotion or an idea.

For example, what is a Vocal Gesture that expresses grief? (Make sure to distinguish between a Behavioral Vocal Gesture for grief, which might be the sound of a sob or a wail, and an Expressive one, which might be an elongated high "eeeeeeeeeeeeey" followed by a deep low "oh . . . ooooh.") What is a Vocal Gesture that expresses Freedom? Terror? What about a Vocal Gesture that expresses the idea of Balance? Or Justice? Or Home?

Behavioral. Just as with Physical Viewpoints, Behavioral Vocal Gestures are of everyday observed life, whether public or private, and give concrete information regarding a person's time, place, condition or character, as well as express specific meaning or intention.

1. Produce a series of Behavioral Vocal Gestures which people around you are making every day on the street, bus or subway, etc. These might include clearing the throat, swallowing, exhaling, sniffing, etc.

2. Produce a series of Behavioral Vocal Gestures that give information about the weather (teeth chattering) or a person's health (coughing) or their age (wheezing).
3. Produce a series of Behavioral Vocal Gestures that express or give information about a person's personality or demeanor, for example, grinding teeth, constant clucking or light whistling.
4. Produce a series of Behavioral Vocal Gestures that have a thought or intention behind them but do not use words. For example, a loud, purposeful clearing of the throat: "eh-hem," a "tsk-tsk" reprimand, a moan expressing pleasure.

EXERCISE 7: ARCHITECTURE

Returning to the three-syllable gibberish word, use it repeatedly, and in different volumes, to explore the physical space in which you are working. This is exactly what a sound technician or a singer does when standing onstage, clapping her/his hands to listen for how *live* or *dead* the room is. Explore corners, walls, their varying textures and materials, distance, objects, etc.

Continuing in Groups

EXERCISE 8: REPETITION

1. The group sits in a circle. Two people go into the center of the circle. Person A is the leader and Person B is the repeater. Using a three-syllable gibberish word, Person A generates a series of sounds using pitch, dynamic, tempo and duration in an Expressive fashion. Person B repeats exactly.
2. Same as above, except Person B switches one Viewpoint while repeating the others exactly. Start with repeating pitch (high to low) but changing dynamic (quiet to loud). For example, if A's word is "X-Y-Z" and s/he says it: X (high and quiet), Y (high and quiet), Z (low and loud); B might

repeat the pitch but change the dynamic by uttering: X (high and loud), Y (high and loud), Z (low and quiet). Continue playing with this until the person following is able to respond spontaneously and playfully.

3. Same as above, except Person B does exact repetition on dynamic, and switches choice of pitch. This exercise can continue or be refined with any combination of Vocal Viewpoints (i.e., repeat pitch and dynamic but switch tempo, etc.).

4. Reverse roles, with B now generating and A repeating.

EXERCISE 9: KINESTHETIC RESPONSE, SILENCE AND ONWARD . . .

Four people sit in the center of a circle with their eyes closed. Each chooses a word, either gibberish or not, as per the leader's discretion. The leader also may give one word or phrase with which the whole group works. By excluding the option of variety in words, and by wholly focusing on the stimuli provided by others, each individual concentrates not on *what* sound s/he produces but on *when*. The *timing* is determined by responding kinesthetically to the sounds of the others.

Note: This exercise closely parallels Lane Work in Physical Viewpoints in that there is a limited vocabulary (the chosen word or phrase), a small group of participants and, therefore, an opportunity to practice a true surrender of control in favor of simple, direct reaction to the external action, in this case sound. Just as *stillness* functions in Physical Viewpoints, so does silence function here. The participants might need to be reminded to include and trust the silences in a proactive, creative fashion rather than a passive one. Silence becomes less an inactive period of waiting than an Expressive field of sound all its own.

THE NEXT STEP

Incorporating Dialogue

EXERCISE 1: SPEAKING AND BREATHING

1. Divide the participants into two groups: A and B. Have each group sit across from each other in a circle. Introduce a piece of dialogue to be memorized on the spot, ideally six to twelve lines of text that are concise and open in their meaning. An example, dialogue of Sarah and Richard from Harold Pinter's play *The Lover*:

   A: Richard?

   B: Mmn?

   A: Do you ever think about me at all . . . when you're with her?

   B: Oh, a little. Not much. We talk about you.

   A: You talk about me with her?

   B: Occasionally. It amuses her.

   A: Amuses her?

   B: Mmnn.

   A: How . . . do you talk about me?

   B: Delicately.

   The A and B groups learn this text first as a chorus through accumulation, adding the next line with each round. For instance, have all the A's say in unison, "Richard?" Then add the B's line, "Mmn?" which they say in unison. Go back and repeat these two lines, this time teaching and adding the third, "Do you ever think about me at all . . ." and so forth. As they learn the text they should also learn to breathe while their partner is speaking, i.e., while the A's speak, the B's inhale; and while the B's speak, the A's inhale.

2. Ask one A and one B to speak the dialogue once through with special attention and responsiveness to what the other initiates. Once the couple has spoken the text through, ask

them to do it again, only differently. Then ask the same couple to accomplish the task in a completely new way. In this particular exercise, you are consciously asking for variety simply for variety's sake (unlike in the early Viewpoints training, where an imposed attempt at variety is discouraged). Encourage differentiation. Allow for arbitrariness.

Notice the narrow limitations in range and how quickly a psychological interpretation can eliminate the potential for spontaneity and play. Are the vocal choices really a response to the other person? How much of the speaking seems premeditated or automatic? When the actors are truly sensitized to each other's choices and adjustments, then the work really begins.

It is valuable for several couples to try this Pinter dialogue with one another to experience the necessity of listening and responding, and for others to observe differences in attack and vocal flexibility in the interactions.

Adding Vocal Viewpoints to Dialogue Work

Now it is time to incorporate the Vocal Viewpoints one at a time. When introducing each Vocal Viewpoint, ask a different couple to try out the dialogue while focusing on the particular Viewpoint in question. Eventually all the Vocal Viewpoints can be in play together (much like Physical Viewpoints, once each is mastered). But initially, concentrate on each Vocal Viewpoint one at a time.

EXERCISE 1: PITCH

Pitch is the level of a sound in the scale, defined by its frequency. As with singing or playing a musical instrument, Pitch is where a sound lies within the possible range of the instrument, in this case, the voice. In Vocal Viewpoints a choice is made about where a note is placed in the vocal range, from low to high or high to low. How wide is the pitch range of each participant? How flexible and able to respond and adjust is the participant to her/his partner's pitch? The person who begins the dialogue above initiates with a particular pitch with as much clarity and exactitude as possible. Thereafter, the choice of pitch at any given moment is always a response to the pitch in play.

EXERCISE 2: DYNAMIC

In Vocal Viewpoints, Dynamic is volume, or the loudness of any given sound. Dynamic is an expression of the degree of aggression or attack by the speaker. Notice how a simple change in Dynamic can radically change the meaning of a moment or interaction. Again, the choice of dynamic should emerge as a response to the dynamic offered by a scene partner.

EXERCISE 3: TEMPO

As in Physical Viewpoints, Tempo is speed. In the case of Vocal Viewpoints, Tempo is the speed with which the words or sounds are expressed. Attention to tempo variation and responsiveness to a partner's tempo are essential. One responds to the other's tempo with a choice of tempo. Notice how Tempo can also alter the meaning of the dialogue and the feel of the relationship expressed in speaking the dialogue.

EXERCISE 4: ACCELERATION/DECELERATION

Ask an A/B couple to accelerate the speed of the dialogue together, starting slow and growing faster, maintaining an acceleration, never leveling out. Once this is possible, try the opposite direction—deceleration—by starting fast, and together collaborating on bringing the speed slower toward the end of the dialogue. How wide can the range of speed be? Can the fast start *very fast* and the slow end *very slowly*? Notice again how Acceleration and

Deceleration alter the meaning of dialogue as well as our perception of Relationship.

EXERCISE 5: REPETITION

With an acute sensitivity to Repetition, participants should play with their partner's pitch, dynamic or tempo through Repetition. Musicians use Repetition to create melodies. Actors can use Repetition as one of the ways they communicate with one another.

EXERCISE 6: TIMBRE

Shape, size and substance determine the particular timbre of any musical instrument. For example, the sound an oboe makes is created by the kind of wood it is made from and by the cavity created by its shape. Opera singers are often renowned for their particular sound, their timbre. The particular physical resonators, the shape and substance of their bodies and lungs determine a singer's distinctive sound. Actors should experiment with producing sound from various physical resonators, nasal, deep-throated, belly, etc., depending upon the character and the situation the character is facing.

EXERCISE 7: SILENCE

The composer John Cage said that a sound is only as loud as the silence on either side of it. Even more than stillness in Physical Viewpoints, Silence offers an incredibly powerful tool for expression; we should acknowledge it, experiment with it and exploit it. Rather than a series of unconscious and random pauses, Silence gains meaning when it is intentional and aesthetically placed. Try dialogue where the two participants choose only one silence. Do not choose the space between the partners' lines for the silence, but rather find it within sentences or in the middle of words. Experiment with how Silence, when placed specifically and sparingly, can create or alter meaning.

Work with the above dialogue, making sure that A inhales during B's lines so that s/he is able to speak right on the tail of B's line, and vice versa; there should be no unintentional interruption of the flow of the dialogue. In life, as people speak together, there is a flow and often an overlapping. Silences are meaningful because they are rare and emerge from the specificity of the situation. Actors too often take their necessary inhale *after* their partner's line, before they begin to speak. They either prepare to speak before doing so, or act before their own line rather than *on* it. This slight break stops the flow of energy. The dialogue becomes "taking turns talking," which can never be truly spontaneous, unpredictable or dynamic.

The act of speaking, according to general anthropology, was born as an act of survival—sound signaled danger; it announced hunger and sexual need. Speaking remains, at best (onstage and in our culture), an act of survival. Speaking is a physical act, not a psychological one. Work with the notion that onstage one must speak from necessity: when all else is physically signaled and expressed, one speaks. See what happens if speaking becomes the *final* stage of the physical necessity to express or communicate.

Watch out for habitual *catch-breaths*: breaths taken involuntarily that stop the flow of words. The habitual catch breaths usually occur from disconnection and fear when one doesn't know the words or doesn't *mean* them enough.

Incorporating Movement

EXERCISE 1: SPEAKING FROM SATS POSITION

This exercise finally brings together both the Physical and Vocal Viewpoints.

1. Each participant brings in a short monologue.
2. Ask one person to walk to center stage, stand in Sats Position (see Chapter 6, page 73) and speak loudly, placing the

first inhalation after the beginning of the monologue as late as possible in the text. Be sure that as s/he runs out of breath, an attempt is made to get louder rather than softer toward the end of the breath. Listen for the results. At which moment, as one begins to lose air, does speaking become physical and necessary? How often do the unconscious *catch-breaths* interfere with the flow of the words?

3. Have seven to nine participants stand in Sats Position, in a horizontal line upstage, left to right, each with a prepared monologue.

4. One begins to speak her/his text. At the moment of the person's first inhalation, another person must begin to speak and the previous person must stop. Only one person at a time should ever be speaking in this exercise. At each inhalation, any other person may take over speaking. The objective is for all participants to get through their entire text once.

This exercise demands an intense listening and awareness of breath. One always picks up where s/he last left off until the monologue is completed. Once everyone has completed her/his monologue, an Open Viewpoints session may follow, while maintaining the Sats line upstage. At any moment, while in Sats, a participant may speak any part of her/his monologue or fragments of someone else's. As always, maintain an attention to the whole, to what is seen and heard by those not participating (the audience).

It is also possible to remove the Sats Position in the middle of Open Viewpoints, and instead have people speak *as* they move in Physical Viewpoints. This is a good way to put the Physical and Vocal Viewpoints together for the first time.

EXERCISE 2: THE CHAIR PIECE

1. Divide everyone into two groups again (A and B). Form A/B couples. Each couple should know both parts of the Pinter text by heart.

2. Have a couple go onstage with a chair and demonstrate for the others. The architecture for this work is simply the chair and roughly eight square feet around the chair. The chair remains where it is during the course of this piece. The context for the couple's movement is the behavior one might generate in a kitchen in the middle of the night. The couple explores a relationship in trouble and the dynamics of being drawn together and yet pulled apart. It is important not to discuss this relationship; rather, find it in the doing.

3. Start the couple in a beginning position; one that through where and how they are positioned physically expresses something of the tension in a relationship. For example, A sits on the chair, hand on one knee, staring off into the distance, and B, back turned, hands on hips, faces upstage. The couple's use of Shape and Spatial Relationship expresses something of the relationship. We will call this *zero position*, as it is simply the point from which we are starting.

4. Once the zero position is established and clear, ask the couple (working together with Viewpoints) to find another position, which is a brand-new tableau expressing a further aspect of the relationship. We'll call this 1 position. Once 1 is clear, make sure the couple can move smoothly from zero to 1.

5. Now go on to 2. Make a new tableau expressing a further dynamic of the relationship.

6. Once 2 is clear move on to 3, and so forth until 7.

7. Once 7 is completed (8 tableaux, or positions, have been completed in all—zero to 7), ask the couple to move through these 8 positions together, this time playing them as a scene. Although the movement must stay the same, the interpretation of the movement changes by how the two actors handle time together. They respond Kinesthetically with attention to Tempo and Duration. They find the meaning of the scene by how they play together.

8. Ask the couple to perform the sequence several times, simply altering their timing, using Kinesthetic Response, Tempo and Duration. Each version should now tell a new story and create new dimensions of relationship, arrived at organically.

9. Now have all the A/B couples come up with their own zero through 7 tableaux, also based on the dynamics of their own couple in a kitchen. They should work without speaking much, except to count their tableaux. They should concentrate on the details and subtleties of the moves, using their experience with Viewpoints to find solutions.

10. Once all the A/B couples have set the sequence, and only after every move is secure, ask them to find a way to place the Pinter text "on top" of the sequence without changing the moves to suit the text. Make sure they simply allow the text to float on top of the movement. Call them on it if (when) they begin to muscle the text or force acting beats.

11. Encourage the couples to discover moments based simply on the combination of what line is spoken with what physical action. Allow a little time for this task, and then ask the couples, one at a time, to perform their chair pieces for the rest of the group.

   Notice how the co-incidental juxtaposition of the text and the movement actually serves to clarify one another (see Durrenmatt reference, Chapter 15, page 187). Notice how the actors are no longer playing a psychology, but rather are playing *with* one another. They leave the conclusions to the viewers. Notice how speed and attack change meaning.

EXERCISE 3: ACTION AND SPEAKING

1. Divide the group into couples.

2. Give each couple the following five actions: (1) overcome a resistance; (2) catch; (3) bow; (4) kiss; (5) run off. Ask each couple to create a movement piece using these five actions in any order.

3. Once they have completed a sketch, ask the couples to intersperse their previous monologues (from Exercise 1, Speaking from Sats Position) within the set action, so that they are speaking dialogue while moving.

4. Each couple should perform its movement/speaking sequences for the whole group one at a time. Note how, when the speaking emerges from and is connected to the physical action (as opposed to remaining separate from it), the text becomes passionate and personal.

This exercise demonstrates how powerful it is to *speak from the actual physical experience.*

Imagine you have just experienced a car crash. You get out of the wrecked car, walk precariously down the road, find a person who might help, and say the following words: "I was just in a car crash!" You would probably not *shout*: "I was just in a car crash!" From the heat of the experience of the car crash, which lives freshly in the body, you speak with necessity, economy and in union to the event. You do not need to shout or prove anything. The recent experience is connected to the act of speaking.

> Do you feel fear and run from the bear or does the act of running generate the feeling of fear?
>
> —JEAN-JACQUES ROUSSEAU

In acting we can learn to rely less on generating feeling out of *thin air*, and instead start trusting the simple physical actions that we live through onstage.

EXERCISE 4: PERSONAL MATERIAL

1. Each participant chooses a memory of a real event that still elicits a sting of emotion. Perhaps the memory triggers a sense of loss or intense happiness.
2. Each person should then create a chain of physical action that embodies the actual remembered event. For example, at a train station you are bidding farewell to a loved one:

blow a kiss and wave, turn, walk off looking one time over your shoulder.

3. Once the physical action is determined, ask a participant to perform that action sequence, imbued with her/his personal experience. Note how physical action is a container for feeling.

4. Now ask all the participants, one at a time, to speak their memories while moving through their own physical action, all the while sustaining the memory and its effect.

5. Next, group the participants into couples. Have each couple turn its solo actions and monologues into scenes by splicing them together.

6. Each couple presents its completed scene, one couple at a time, for the others.

Note: This particular exercise results in spontaneity and a lack of self-consciousness, because the participants are being asked to juggle so many things at once: physical action, speaking, inhabiting a memory, and a relationship with a partner. It is impossible to *think* your way through this exercise. There is simply too much going on.

The multiplication of tasks in these exercises may seem overwhelming but is, in fact, designed to allow intuition to kick in and overtake some of the more limiting and controlling mechanisms of the brain.

CHAPTER 10

VIEWPOINTS IN REHEARSAL

The most commonly asked question about Viewpoints is: "How do I use this in rehearsing a play?" The application of Viewpoints training to the rehearsal process is complex and changes according to the material, the director's and/or playwright's point of view and the dynamics of the cast.

Viewpoints training can be incorporated throughout all the stages of the rehearsal process and has a wide range of benefits.

- During the *first stages of rehearsal* it can be used to (1) create an ensemble and (2) develop a physical vocabulary for the world of the play.
- In the *second stages of rehearsal* it can be used to (1) deepen character, (2) find the physical life for the play and (3) apply directly to the staging of scenes or transitions.
- During the *running of a show* it can be used to (1) provide a company warm-up and (2) maintain freshness and spontaneity in performance.

EARLY REHEARSALS

It is best to incorporate Viewpoints training into the early rehearsal process, even on the first day of a project. In working with very experienced actors, or perhaps somewhat protected actors, make a point of asking the group to be open, to allow for play, mistakes, intimacy and embarrassment. It is helpful to say something like: "You don't have to like this or agree with it, but I ask that, for today, you approach the work with an open heart." Introduced with sensitivity, passion and clarity, Viewpoints training always breaks down barriers of resistance—and quickly.

Applying Viewpoints training at the start of the rehearsal process is an excellent way to take in new bodies, in a new time, in a new space, on a new piece. When working with a new group, you should always introduce the individual Viewpoints in a simple fashion, following basic guidelines (see Chapters 1 and 2), even if one or more participants are already experienced with the practice. Our suggestion is to first move through the basic introduction of Viewpoints, including the individual Viewpoints, *soft focus*, Grid Work, Lane Work and Open Viewpoints.

In the first several days of rehearsal, Viewpoints training is primarily used to create an ensemble, establish a shortcut vocabulary and establish a physical vocabulary.

Create an Ensemble

By having a group work in close (sweaty) physical contact, Viewpoints training quickly breaks down barriers of politeness and individual fears by encouraging individuals to bust through, loosen up, play. It's the difference between dipping your toes in the water and plunging in—Viewpoints is a plunge, a way to get the group functioning *as a group*. Value is placed on listening and responding to others. Pressure is released from any one person who feels that they have to create in a vacuum. Emphasis is placed on the fact that the piece will be made by and belong to everyone in the ensemble—there are no small roles. Very often, if the play is not ensemble in nature, these sessions become one, if not the only, opportunity for the company to be together and work together as a company until the beginning of tech and/or performances. (Participants have often commented that were it not for Viewpoints, they might never have known that so-and-so was in the same show.)

Establish a Shortcut Spoken Vocabulary

Once the terminology of Viewpoints is introduced, it can remain a shortcut for giving direction or asking for adjustment throughout the entire process. If you are working with ten people onstage, rather than taking five minutes to say: "John, move downstage right about a foot, no upstage a bit more, good . . ." or "Now Sarah, take a step to your left . . . no, just one step . . ." you can simply say: "Spatial Relationship" and the group will instantly adjust themselves into more powerful expressive relationships and stage pictures. Naming ways to talk about time and space onstage leads to a shared language, a common vocabulary. This saves time and circumvents misunderstanding.

Establish a Physical Vocabulary for the Play-World

What makes one production different from another? What makes ten actors in one production all seem like they're in the same production, while ten in another are all acting in different plays? What makes a Play-World specific and therefore memorable? The fundamental notion implicit in all our discussion of both Viewpoints and Composition is that there is an actual language in the physical life of a production. There is a spoken text (usually), but there is also a movement and/or imagistic text. As directors and designers and performers, we say things, make statements, create meaning, with the physical life of a production. We need to make our *writing* as specific as we would wish of the playwright. This early work on establishing the vocabulary of a Play-World is the same as a writer collecting phrases or research, a painter choosing the colors for the palette, a composer exploring feels (or fields) before any of the specifics are set in stone. Not all paintings include all colors; even a piece of baroque music is identified by distinct characteristics of harmony and meter.

"That's *Vice*."

The producers of the television show *Miami Vice* employed a man whose job it was to meet with whoever was directing that week's episode, go with him/her to scout locations, shop for clothes, etc., and determine if something was or was not "*Vice*." When something belonged in the world of the show, he'd say: "That's *Vice*"; when it didn't, he'd say: "That's not *Vice*."

When working on a production, these early Viewpoint sessions are about leading the group to a collective agreement about what is and what is not "*Vice*" for the particular Play-World.

"Point to it."

If the play is set in a particular period or place, do Open Viewpoints with that setting as a theme. Images and patterns and textures will appear that you should note and then point out to the company. As the philosopher Wittgenstein said: "If you can't say it, point to it." A picture of the thing to be created will slowly emerge. It will include certain things (maybe swirling topography, maybe people on the floor, maybe slow tempos) and it will exclude others. Feel free to point to things that are *not* of the Play-World and explain why.

If you are creating a piece with an invented Play-World you will begin to define it. How does time work here? What unexpected opposites go together?

Very often, we cannot put into exact words what a piece should look like, move like, feel like. Sometimes we don't even know ourselves. But we know it when we see it. We know what moves us and excites us.

So, let's say you are going into rehearsal for a production of Elmer Rice's *The Adding Machine* or the 1950s musical *The Boy Friend*, which is set in the 1920s. You might do Open Viewpoints by dropping in "The 1920s." Have half the company work, the other half watch. When you're done, ask the group that watched to say what they observed—not good or bad, but simply what emerged. What topography did the actors work on? What shapes were repeated? What gestures? You might note fast tempos, geometric shapes, *isolation* of body parts. Then discuss whether the patterns that emerged are or are not "*Vice*," or rather: "That's *Adding Machine*" or "That's *Boy Friend*," and why.

"Anything is possible."

As discussed earlier, Viewpoints can free an actor from the belief that: "My character would never do that." Viewpoints is a tool for discovering action, not from psychology or backstory, but from immediate physical stimuli. Actors and directors should watch the company Viewpoint, and note not only the moments that are obviously in the play, but those that *could* be. As directors, we can be just as narrow-minded in saying: "My play would never include that." Viewpoints is your gift for exploding the envelope, working outside the box, finding more unexpected choices, remaining open to what happens and what stirs you, rather than what you originally thought should and should not. Consider everything.

By observing emerging patterns in Viewpoints, you will be able to develop what we call an *Ingredients List*. Keep a list of what occurs time and again and is of your Play-World. Keep a list of what persists and resonates. Let these impressions form the foundation of your Ingredients List: the possible items you might use to create your mixture (in this case the production). These might include very specific gestures, types of movement, or actual sequences you will later incorporate into the production. (The Ingredients List is discussed in greater detail in the next chapter.)

MIDDLE STAGES

In the early to middle stages of rehearsal you start to address if, and how, you would like to apply Viewpoints to the specifics of the text (assuming there is one). The exercises in which View-points training is most useful in terms of approaching text, character and scene work are explored more completely in Composition exercises (Chapters 11–15) rather than Viewpoint exercises. But here are some general exercises that can help bridge the gap between the open quality of the Viewpoints and the concrete nature of the text.

The Play

You can Viewpoint with any word or directive as a stimulus— we'll call this the *seed*. The word or phrase you drop in for the group is meant to be only a starting point, out of which something will evolve.

For example, in working on Chekhov, you might begin Open Viewpoints with the *seed* of: "Russia" or "The Gentry" or "Memory" or "Making Theater" or "Unspoken Passion."

Add specifics as desired; for instance a confined space in which to work, a given circumstance, or character assignments.

Character

EXERCISE 1: OPEN VIEWPOINTS "IN CHARACTER"

Begin Open Viewpoints. Have the company drop in the idea of character. Let "who they are" influence their continuing work.

Encourage them to let things emerge, rather than *play at* or *illustrate*. They do not need to walk or behave differently, only become aware of how the idea of their character might subtly shift their choices of tempo (Does this person move fast or slow?), their relationship to architecture (Does the person hug walls or thrive in the center of open space?), and so on. Maintain awareness of the individual Viewpoints and continue to work off others. When you stop the Viewpoints work, discuss what relationships emerged *between* people. Did the participants find themselves close to certain individuals, far from others? Were there comfort zones and danger zones?

For further exploration, select a small number of people to do Open Viewpoints in character. Have them choose distinct or heated *relationships* from the world of the play you are rehearsing: a group of four who are blood relations, a couple who is falling in love, two groups at war with each other.

Repeat the above, but within a given *setting*. You can choose a doorway or stairwell, you can choose to give them one chair and five feet of playing space.

Repeat the above (with the same or different characters), but add a *situation* or *circumstance*. You can state that it is late on a cold winter's night, you can state that they all want to leave but only one of them can.

EXERCISE 2: LIFE STORY TOPOGRAPHY FOR CHARACTER

Just as each individual worked on creating her/his own life story through Topography (see Chapter 5, Additional Exercises for Focusing on Individual Viewpoints, Exercise 6), now each individual does the same for a character in the play (or the one s/he is playing; this is the director's choice). Give them five to ten minutes to work on and develop their sequence of floor patterns. Each individual presents her/his movement piece for the group.

EXERCISE 3: ELEMENTS OF A CHARACTER PORTRAIT, OR THE HOT SEAT (TWO PARTS)

It's useful to do this exercise earlier rather than later in the rehearsal process, ideally before or just as the actors get on their feet for the first time. For some, this will feel premature. They might insist that they don't know anything about who their characters are yet, and that making choices now will be limiting later. It's important to stress to the company that you are purposely asking them to approach the work from two very different angles: (1) from the head, by doing text work, discussion, reading the play aloud and (2) from their intuition, dreams and impressions. Let them know that for the moment they're supposed to make immediate and rash decisions, and that nothing they say today must be true tomorrow.

This exercise can be developed by the director to include some, all, or none of the following specified questions. Choose what is most useful for your particular play and company. And, if interested, you can use what the actors come up with later in Composition work, by having them combine the separate elements they create here into a full Composition: a Character Composition (see Chapter 13, Exercise 4).

Part I: Writing

Gather the group together in a circle, each with pad and pencil. Ask them to complete a series of personal statements about their character (sample statements and responses are below). They should write down the entire sentence as you state it, then fill in the blanks; when they read their answers back later, they must answer with the full statement exactly as it was posed to them. Give them a tiny bit less time for each question than you think they need to answer it thoughtfully; create *Exquisite Pressure* by reducing time and increasing spontaneity.

As your character, fill in these statements:

My name is _____.

I am _____ years old.

I am from _____.

My profession is _____.

Five facts I know from the text are:

I am a student.
I am single.
My father just passed away.
I take long walks.
I say, "Excuse me," frequently.

Five things I intuit (but which are not stated in the text) are:

I sleep poorly at night.
I'm afraid of being alone.
I laugh in a high cackle.
My favorite color is blue.
I'm embarrassed by my height.

A telling action I perform in the play is _____.

A telling line I speak is _____.

My greatest fear is _____.

My greatest longing is _____.

Odd habits I have are _____.

My likes include _____.

My dislikes include _____.

Part 2: Moving

After you've finished with the questions from above, and before you read them aloud, get the company to work on their feet. State out loud to them the following list of movements, which they need to generate on their own, and give them five to ten minutes to prepare:

- An action with Tempo that expresses character
- An action with Duration that expresses character
- A floor pattern that expresses character
- Three Behavioral Gestures that are particular to the character's personality, culture, time or place
- Two Expressive Gestures that express the essence of character, a propelling force or a conflict within
- A walk across the room with bold choices regarding Tempo, Shape and Topography.

Gather the group back together and sit as an audience. Ask one individual at a time to get up into the *hot seat* and share her/his statements and movement, in exactly the way you ordered it, with the exact wording. For instance, the individual should say, "My name is Blanche DuBois," then go on to state her age, etc., ending with (as a completed example), "My dislikes include naked light bulbs, etc." When each participant performs her/his movement, s/he should state the name; for instance, s/he should announce, "Tempo," then perform the action, then "Duration," etc., making sure there is a clear start and finish to each action, returning to neutral in between.

Alternative: Have cast members work on and present a character that someone else is playing, instead of the character they have been cast to play.

SCENE WORK

EXERCISE 1: VIEWPOINTS AND TEXT

Scene partners Viewpoint off each other. They can work with or without text. Primary focus is on the individual Viewpoints, with the text floating on top of the movement. "No acting, please" is the operative here, until the movement organically and inevitably begins to inform the action and lead to emotional choices. (See more on this in Chapter 9, Speaking from Sats Position, Exercise 1, page 115.)

EXERCISE 2: EXPRESSIVE STAGING

Divide the company into groups of scene partners according to who plays with whom in the text. A group might end up having two people or twenty. Have each group create a sequence of movement that expresses one of the following three assigned topics:

1. The essence of their relationship to each other.
2. The essence of their relationship to the space.
3. The blocks of action in a particular scene.

For this, break the scene down into three to five sections, and give each section a title, as if it were a chapter in a book. Create movement that expresses the essence of the title for each section. For instance: "The Arrival," "Cat and Mouse," "The Fight Begins" and "Left Alone" might be the chapter titles of a given scene. The movement should not be illustrative and bound by the details of the scene. The point of the titles is to translate the action of the scene into larger, more schematic or iconographic ideas.

The sequence of movement should use all the individual Viewpoints, and should consist of five to ten moves (you can assign any number). Each group should refine and repeat their sequence until it is set. The movement should be Expressive rather than descriptive.

Next, one group performs their movement for the other groups. At this point, based on your careful observation of where this particular group is and what would be helpful, you can choose one of the following four options:

1. Have the group repeat the form of the movement, but play with different Tempos and Duration, with extreme awareness of Kinesthetic Response (shifts in timing will not change *what* is performed but *how* it is performed; see the Pinter exercise in Chapter 9).
2. Have the group repeat the movement while adding text. The text should *float* on the movement rather than muscle it into something new. Pay attention to how the meaning of lines and acting beats change by the physical action with which it is aligned. This provides an immediate explosion of expectations around a scene. When you work on nonillustrative movement completely separate from the text and then put the movement and text together, the possibilities of a scene explode open.
3. Have the group incorporate the text with their movement, as above, and then continue through the rest of the scene using Open Viewpoints.
4. Without any text at first, have the group begin their movement and make a fluid transition into Viewpointing off each other when they get to the end of their set sequence. As they are working, at any point when you feel that they are completely connected and listening to each other's bodies, have them add text and thus begin the scene, without decreasing any awareness of Viewpoints.

Have each group work in this fashion, and with your guidance. When all groups have gone, discuss what emerged as possibilities for your production.

STAGING

Viewpoints training can be used to create staging (blocking) for a production. For both actor and director, Viewpoints is a pathway to unexpected choices not dictated by text, psychology or intention. This does not mean that Viewpoints is incompatible with other approaches to acting, only that it provides an alternative and a compliment. For instance, one of the most rewarding applications of Viewpoints training for Tina has been at the Steppenwolf summer program in Chicago, where a three-hour daily Viewpoints class is followed by a Meisner technique class taught by Steppenwolf ensemble member Amy Morton. While the means are different, we have discovered that the ends of both techniques are very much the same: to be in the moment, to listen, to respond to what your partner gives you.

A reminder: Viewpoints does not imply a style. The work produced by Viewpoints can be highly formal and choreographic or highly naturalistic and behavioral. To one extreme, you can use Viewpoints to find movement that you then set, independently from the text (as stated above). The text is put together with the set movement to create tension and juxtaposition. The text and movement become highly legible through their *difference* from each other. To the other extreme, you can simply rehearse a scene while maintaining awareness of the individual Viewpoints. People talk, sit, drink coffee, play cards, etc., while taking care of Spatial Relationship . . . while having a sense of Duration . . . while using Architecture . . .

Of course directors constantly make choices, conscious or not, involving Viewpoints, most obviously in their blocking, which utilizes Architecture and Topography. (For more thoughts on Viewpoints and directing, see Chapter 17.) If you are directing, ask yourself: What *is* the staging in this piece? Is it the way we observe people in *real life*? Am I staging a replication, a documentary, a commentary? Is it someone's dream, a hallucination, a fantasy? Is it an expression of one character's feeling? Or a memory from a particular point of view? Is it a diatribe or a plea?

Have the participants create movement, using Viewpoints, which accomplishes any or all of the below:

- Re-creates behavior
- Expresses relationship
- Exposes subtext
- Heightens conflict
- Operates from one character's point of view.

Different aspects of the play will be revealed by "staging" from different points of view. There will inevitably be numerous possibilities that arise here. Think of all movement that is created here as being communal property. The company is collectively coming up with as many options and approaches as possible. The movement they generate is yours to edit, shape or use in another section.

FOR FURTHER REHEARSAL

After a scene is fully rehearsed and staged, ask the performers to run the scene while paying heightened attention to the individual Viewpoints. They should pick up on things of which they were previously unaware: little beats, movement, breaths, turns of the head. Invite them to adjust and change within the scene, in response to the new information they are perceiving.

Or, if you want to work on a given section, or if you are stuck, begin to Viewpoint. Stop the company when something useful occurs. Ask them to repeat and refine it. Then move on to the next little chunk of material. In this way you can also make modules of material that can be cut and pasted in other ways later.

VIEWPOINTS IN PERFORMANCE

Neither one of us has ever done a production consisting entirely of Open and *unplanned* Viewpoints. This work would be closer to what we call improvisation.

In our experience, Viewpoints training has been invaluable for maintaining freshness in the long run of shows. Viewpoints asks the actors to remain constantly awake. Although the form is more or less repeated night to night, the "how it is filled" certainly changes and, even more importantly, what actors are given by their partner(s) is never the same. Viewpoints trains actors to remain awake to the most subtle shifts of their partners.

The stories of actors who have gotten offstage only to be told about an accident that occurred upstage right behind them . . . or who didn't hear the siren outside . . . or, maybe worse, who were paying so much attention to the siren outside that they did not notice their scene partner's adjustment . . . or of the actors who say their lines exactly the same way night after night while the world shifts seismically around them—these are the wonders and pitfalls of being onstage without awareness.

CHAPTER 11

INTRODUCING
COMPOSITION

Composition is a natural extension of Viewpoints training. It is the act of writing as a group, in time and space, using the language of the theater. Participants create short pieces for the stage by putting together raw material into a form that is repeatable, theatrical, communicative and dramatic. The process of creating Compositions is by nature collaborative: within a short amount of time, participants arrive at solutions to certain delineated tasks. These solutions, arranged and performed as a piece, are what constitute a Composition. The creative process demands cooperation and quick, intuitive decisions. It is possible to use the principals of Physical and Vocal Viewpoints while constructing these Compositions.

Compositions can be centered on particular plays or can be used for generating original work based on a theme or an idea or a hunch. Composition work functions the way sketching does for a painter: Compositions, created from ideas sketched in time and space, introduce notions that may be useful for a given production.

EXQUISITE PRESSURE
AND SUBJECTIVE TIME

The key to Composition work is to do a lot in a little time. When we are not given the time to think or talk too much (because someone has set a time limit), wonderful work often emerges; what surfaces does not come from analysis or ideas, but from our impulses, our dreams, our emotions. All kinds of pressure affect the rehearsal process of a production: opening night, critics, friends and family, etc. These pressures are rarely freeing or constructive. Exquisite Pressure comes from an environment where forces lean on the participants in a way that enables more, not less, creativity. Exquisite Pressure comes from an attitude of necessity and respect for the people with whom you're working, for the amount of time you have, for the room you work in, for what you're doing with all of these.

When a Composition assignment is given, it's always important to remind the groups not to spend their time sitting and discussing and planning. From the start, they should get up on their feet and begin. Whenever groups are spread out working on their own assignments, you can always tell where the stuck people are—they are invariably sitting in a circle, looking at their pieces of paper, either all talking at once or no one talking at all, as they try to "come up with ideas." You can always spot the group where the juices are flowing: they look like kids in a playground. They are usually running around, with one person shouting: "I'll get the broom!" Or someone leaping up and down in the air, saying: "Oooh oooh, oooh, I got it! I got it!" Or two people talking over each other at once with: "Yes!" and "What if . . ."

What are the conditions necessary to create Exquisite Pressure for your group? Give them just enough time in the Composition assignment to create something they can own and repeat (so it's not just improv and accident), but not so much time that they can stop to think or judge even for an instant. It's often useful to say: "You have twenty minutes—go." And then wait it out. See how the groups are fairing. They will never know that your watch runs on *subjective time*. If they look like they are close to finishing, give them a "one-minute" warning. Push them. If twenty minutes have actually passed and they're still in the heat of something really going on, and need more time, give them "another five," etc. Pay attention and keep the pressure on.

Exquisite Pressure is also created by giving just the right amount of ingredients for the assignment (not too few, not too many), putting the proper number of people in each group, and determining the complexity of the assignment. There should be levels of difficulty with which you begin and to which you graduate. But in all cases, the challenge needs to be great enough, the stakes high enough, for the group to enter into a state of spontaneous play.

In determining how to create a successful Composition assignment, how high to turn on the heat, etc., consider: numbers, leader vs. collective, ingredients, complexity and preparation time.

Numbers

The number of people in each group. Early on, it's useful to begin Composition work with three to five people in a group, and grow from there. (Once, when Tina was finishing a three-week training program at Steppenwolf, she gave a Composition assignment to the entire group, made up of twenty-five individuals working together.)

Leader Vs. Collective, Including: "Yes, and . . ."

Whether or not there is a leader or director elected in each group. In early Composition work, it's often best not to have one person in a more dominant position than the others. One of the gifts of Composition is the way in which it asks us to become authentic collaborators, to work with a spirit of generosity. If a group is working together, listening to each other, not worrying about power and control, the work is usually fantastic. When a group begins assessing and arguing, the work stalls. The ability to be open to whatever is offered by others is called: *"Yes, and . . ."* Encourage each member of the group to say: "Yes, and . . ." as opposed to: "No, but . . ." When someone offers a suggestion, look for what is useful in it and build on it (Yes, and . . .), rather than stressing why it won't work and what should be done instead (No, but . . .). Say: "Let's try it."

There comes a point in Composition work when it is invaluable to have people leading the Compositions. When the time is right, have an individual put her/his unique and personal work out into the world—this *is* Exquisite Pressure. Exquisite Pressure asks someone to unveil herself/himself as an artist, to stand behind what s/he makes, and to learn from what s/he and others see.

When there is a director on a Composition, individuals get less time to practice their "Yes, and . . ." They are not asked as readily to contribute. However, there is a person who can practice the "Yes, and . . ." in this situation—the director. Practice by asking, determine certain things about your Composition and leave other things open, invite contributions and, most importantly, be open to others when they offer their input, even without being asked.

Ingredients

The elements you select to be included in any given composition assignment, and out of which the work will be composed. These might include objects, sounds, physical actions, text, theatrical conventions, etc. The right kind of Exquisite Pressure is created by how many ingredients you assign to be included in the piece and how difficult they are to find, make or include.

Complexity

Expressed in structure and length. A complex assignment, as opposed to a simple one, increases Exquisite Pressure. A Composition that includes three actions and is designed to be one minute in length is obviously more comfortable than a ten-minute piece composed of five different sections, each one with a conflict and resolution. Start easy enough to get your group on fire. As you move forward in Composition work, turn up the heat, so that your group is always flying by the seat of its pants.

Preparation Time

The right amount of time. Determine whether to give the assignment in the moment and send the group off, or assign it the day before. When you assign a director to lead the Composition, it is often useful for you to give her/him the assignment earlier. This allows her/him to determine how much to come in with pre-planned, and how much to concoct in the moment with the ensemble. Whether you preplan or create in the moment, never give so much time that the Exquisite Pressure deflates.

Montage is a way of putting images together that incorporates juxtaposition, contrast, rhythm and story. It creates a through-line by assembling, overlaying and overlapping different materials collected from different sources.

Montage originated with the genesis of film. In the very early days of filmmaking, a heavy camera would be set up and remain static in order to record certain events. For example, a melodrama would be played out in front of the camera, or a fire extinguished by fire trucks and firemen would be filmed from one spot. The camera did not move.

It was pioneer filmmaker D. W. Griffith who first suggested, much to the surprise of his cameraman Billy Bitzer, that the camera be moved closer to the action. This one shocking and innovative movement of the camera gave birth not only to the close-up, but also to *editing* and *point of view*. A sequence showing a firefighter at work juxtaposed with a close-up of a woman watching the action allows the audience to see the fire through the eyes of the woman. The movement of the camera created the necessity for editing. No longer simply a recording device, the camera became a highly articulate and subjective instrument.

The Russian filmmaker Sergei Eisenstein refined editing and montage into an art form through emphasis on rhythm and contrast. A series of edited shots (montage) could incorporate and juxtapose close-ups, pans and long shots, and tell a story in an entirely new way, expressing a subjective point of view. A sequence consisting of a series of dissolves, superimpositions or cuts could condense time or suggest memories or hallucinations. The impact of the story upon the viewer depended upon how disparate shots were put together. This putting-together is what constitutes montage. In film, montage became the primary method of telling a story and remains so to this day.

The theater can use these techniques, substituting physical movement for camera movement and editing. How can you create a close-up or pan or jump-cut without the use of a camera? How can you put together disparate materials into a whole, using the techniques of montage? (For further exploration, see Chapter 16, Composition and Related Arts.)

1. Divide into groups of three. In each group, decide who will be 1, 2 and 3. Each participant will have fifteen minutes to direct the other two group members in a short Composition based on notions of montage.
2. Start the assignment by defining montage and introduce its history and use in film.
3. Decide on the space in which this Composition will take place. Because there are so many people directing and so many Compositions, it is best to determine two distinct areas: one for the stage and another for the audience. Ideally the area chosen to be the stage offers some interesting architecture, such as doors or windows or a balcony.
4. Each participant chooses a personal story or incident about love and loss that still retains a powerful personal relevance. The task of this Composition exercise is to stage an

expression of this story or incident in the form of a five-part montage, within these confines:

- Step 1: Ten minutes for everyone to look carefully at the stage space in order to *storyboard* in a notebook some ideas for their Composition. It is important that each person allow time for the architecture to influence choices, to let the room "speak" and suggest ideas about how it wants to be used and how it can be used to relate this incident.
- Step 2: Fifteen minutes for director 1 to stage a Composition.
- Step 3: Fifteen minutes for director 2 to stage a Composition.
- Step 4: Fifteen minutes for director 3 to stage a Composition.

The structure. Five *shots* or takes, each one a maximum of fifteen seconds long, separated by *blackouts*, during which those in the audience close their eyes. The director can say, for example, "Lights out," and the audience members will close their eyes, and, "Lights up," and the audience members will open their eyes.

It is possible to incorporate minimal props or furniture in the montage Composition, but only when it is necessary to express something particular. It is also possible to use sound or text, but sparingly and with exactitude, not improvised. Every move, every object and every sound should be eloquent.

The following instructions will help each director create her/his montage Composition:

- Within the fifteen minutes of rehearsal try to choreograph the events meticulously, with great attention to detail.
- Work physically. Do not waste time describing the psychology or meaning of the incident to the

actors. Instead, speak with brevity and give physical instructions, such as: "Enter through the door quickly, take five steps, look to the right, exhale, look back slowly while drawing out the word, 'Fire!' in a whisper." Direct from a physical rather than a psychological point of view.

◻ Use the fifteen minutes to stage an *Expression* of the event rather than a *Description* of it. *Describing* an event is staging a replica of it as objectively as possible; *Expressing* an event is staging how it impacted you, what it felt like through a subjective lens. (See Descriptive Vs. Expressive Staging a little further down.)

◻ Once you give instructions, look carefully at what the actors do with them and make adjustments based on what you observe about their contribution. How can you, the leader, use the specific physicality and idiosyncrasies of these particular actors most effectively?

◻ Keep things moving. Work intuitively. Concentrate on details. Work with *exactitude*. Make it matter *where* things happen and *when* they happen.

5. Once all three directors in each group have had fifteen minutes to stage their Compositions, it is time to perform them for the audience (the other groups). Before these performances begin, take a moment for further instruction to the actors (which in this case includes everyone) as well as the directors (also includes everyone).

To the Actors:

◻ Now that the decisions about a series of certain actions have been agreed upon in rehearsal, the performance of these agreements is not just about their proper execution. A performance is only a possibility that something might occur, a meeting, a real human engagement. Use Viewpoints training within this choreographed, set material to remain engaged kinesthetically and aware of how you are handling time together. How does the audience influence the use of time? Try to slow down time and meet one another onstage in front of the audience.

▫ Take care of the *jo-ha-kyu*. Simply stated, the *jo-ha-kyu* is the beginning, middle and end. It is the rhythmic journey of a gesture, an interaction, a story or an event. (See description on page 147.) To "take care of the *jo-ha-kyu*" means that the actors tend to the journey they shape for themselves and for an audience.

▫ Take a curtain call at the end of your group's three Compositions.

To the Directors:

▫ A director has two ensembles: the actors and the audience. Composition work is a chance to practice this dual responsibility. Take care of the audience. Do not assume that they know what to do, when to close their eyes, or what will happen next.

▫ Take care of the audience's *jo-ha-kyu* (see above). Be sensitive to the audience's mood and stamina. Are they tired? Do they need a break from: "Lights out/Lights up"? Is there a way you might help that situation?

▫ Take responsibility for the audience's experience of time and Duration during the Composition. Make sure the blackouts are not too long. It is vital for a director to develop a feel for the audience's experience of time.

▫ Take care of the actors' safety and well-being.

Composition work is a chance for directors to practice their relationship to an audience. An audience can always sense a director's attitude toward and relationship to them even when s/he is not present at the performance. Spectators can sense the director's fear, generosity, carelessness or consideration. Use the Composition exercises to consider the audience's experience, take care of them, give them an access point to enter into your work. Be sensitive to their attention.

DESCRIPTIVE VS. EXPRESSIVE STAGING

In staging a Composition it is possible to stage Descriptively or Expressively. Descriptive staging essentially repeats the external physical and vocal reality of the event being *described*. For example, if you were to stage the night your great love left you, you could try to stage exactly what happened literally (Descriptive), or you could stage what it felt like (Expressive). You could stage a man packing his suitcase and saying good-bye to a woman sitting at a table (Descriptive), or you could stage a man and a woman slowly walking backward away from one another (Expressive).

The sculptor Constantin Brancusi described his attempt to get at the Expressive rather than Descriptive qualities of his art by asking:

> "When you see a fish, you do not think of its scales, do you? You think of its speed, its floating, flashing body seen through water. Well, I've tried to express just that. If I made fins and eyes and scales, I would arrest its movement and hold you by a pattern, or a shape of reality. I want just the flash of its spirit."

JO-HA-KYU

A performance is a flow, which has a rising
and a falling curve.

—PETER BROOK

Zeami, the fifteenth century Japanese founder of Noh theater, wrote *12 Treatises for the Theater*, an astonishing account of his discoveries about acting and theater that are still relevant and applicable today (see Bibliography). One of the fundamental building blocks of Zeami's thought, *jo-ha-kyu* is of particular significance to Viewpoints and Composition.

Jo-ha-kyu is essentially a rhythmic pattern. *Jo-ha-kyu* can be simply translated as "beginning, middle and end." But, in fact, the meaning is much more complex and useful as you look deeper:

Jo = Introduction
Ha = Exposition
Kyu = Denouement.

Or:

Jo = Resistance
Ha = Rupture
Kyu = Acceleration.

Or:

Jo = Hop
Ha = Skip
Kyu = Jump.

Performances of Noh theater, usually presented during the course of a long evening, were composed of three disparate plays: a Noh play (jo), a kyogen or comedy (ha), and another serious Noh play (kyu). Zeami suggests that it is the theater artists' responsibility to attend to the audience's experience or journey throughout the evening. The journey is divided into jo-ha-kyu:

Jo = Introduction
Ha = Breaking
Kyu = Rapid (a gradual increase of pace from slow to fast).

The first play, jo, warms the audience into the evening. Ha breaks the mood of jo; therefore, in Noh, the ha section is the comedy play, or kyogen. The kyu, the other Noh play, accelerates toward the end. These three sections move in an ever-increasing pace and form the basic dramatic, rhythmic and melodic basis of Noh.

Every theater evening has a jo-ha-kyu. But now the theory gets even more interesting:

An evening has a jo-ha-kyu
A play has a jo-ha-kyu
An act of a play has a jo-ha-kyu
A scene has a jo-ha-kyu
An interaction has a jo-ha-kyu
An action has a jo-ha-kyu
A gesture has a jo-ha-kyu.

According to Zeami, every kyu (ending) contains the next jo (beginning); every ending of a gesture contains the beginning of the next gesture.

Once you begin to recognize and experience jo-ha-kyu in action, you are instantly responsible to it. It can be a useful tool in organizing energy and flow of action on the stage:

Jo = Begin in an easy manner
Ha = Develop dramatically
Kyu = Finish rapidly.

A successful production is a great journey. The journey pulls an audience like a magnet. The experience draws you farther along, through trials and rough mountain pathways to sudden clearings and valleys. There are moments to breathe and other moments of tension or dramatic upheaval. There is contraction and expansion.

Listen to the end of a Mahler symphony. Hear how the endings slow down and speed up simultaneously. Mahler was a master of kyu in every piece of music he wrote:

Jo = the initial phase, when the force is put in motion
as if overcoming a resistance

Ha = the transition phase, rupture of the resistance,
increase of the motion

Kyu = the rapid phase, an unbridled crescendo, ending in a sudden stop.

The opposition between a force that tends to increase and another force that holds back determines the first phase: jo (to retain). Ha (to break) happens at the moment when one is freed from the retaining force, and develops until the arrival of the third phase, kyu. In kyu (speeding up), the action climaxes with all its force, then suddenly stops, as if faced with a resistance, when a new jo is ready to start again.

Zeami also addressed the actor's responsibility to the audience in jo-ha-kyu. If a latecomer arrives in the midst of the jo section of the play, Zeami writes, the actor is responsible for bringing the latecomer through the jo and into the ha with the rest of the audience. How different this notion is to our separation of audience in the American theater. Looking at Zeami's writings can only challenge us to make a theater that is more vital.

COMPOSITION ASSIGNMENT 2: TELLING A STORY WITH OBJECTS AND SPATIAL RELATIONSHIPS

1. Each participant directs a Composition on her/his own, using objects as actors.
2. The stage is the top of a table.
3. Tell a story in five tableaux, divided by blackouts, on the tabletop using only the objects. The story should be expressed

by the placement of the objects, their distance from one another and what happens to them simply in the development of Spatial Relationship in the five tableaux.

Allow fifteen minutes for preparation of these Compositions.

In this exercise, think of the tabletop as the entire world. Introducing any object onto the table creates a dramatic situation.

COMPOSITION ASSIGNMENT 3: LOSS/REUNION

1. Divide into groups of four to seven participants. Choose whether or not to assign a director in each group.
2. The groups work site-specifically, searching outside of the normal rehearsal space to find new locations where they might stage and present their pieces.
3. No blackouts are allowed.
4. The Composition should last a maximum of eight minutes and be built on the following structure: (Part 1) The Meeting; (Part 2) Something Happens; (Part 3) Loss; (Part 4) The Reunion.
5. The following ingredients need to be included (in any order) in this Composition:

   □ Revelation of Space
   □ Revelation of Object
   □ Revelation of Character
   □ A sustained moment when everyone is looking up
   □ One element (air, water, fire, earth) used in excess
   □ A reference to a famous painting
   □ A surprise entrance
   □ A sustained passionate kiss
   □ Broken expectations
   □ One gesture repeated fifteen times
   □ A staged accident
   □ Twenty consecutive seconds of stillness

- Fifteen consecutive seconds of top-speed talking
- Fifteen consecutive seconds of unison action
- Fifteen consecutive seconds of sustained laughter
- Sound (other than vocal) used in three contrasting ways, for example: recorded music, live percussion and naturalistic sound effects
- Something sung
- Something very loud
- Six lines of text (the instructor should choose these from any text source, and assign the same lines to all groups; later, as Composition work becomes more complex, you can increase how much text you assign).

This Composition may at first seem like an overload of elements, but it will introduce the basics of a theatrical grammar in an exciting way. Most of the elements are ancient. "Revelation of Space," for example, occurs every time a curtain is drawn open. "Broken expectations" are found in every great story. And so on.

Initially it is useful to work site-specifically in creating Compositions. This means choosing a site outside a traditional theater structure, such as the side of a building, a field or a stairwell. The process of working site-specifically develops a consciousness about architectural and spatial possibilities, which can then be carried by the creator back into a conventional theater space.

Think of found architecture as an actual *set design*, a set perhaps that would be sensationally expensive, perhaps impossible, to build in a theater. Through work with these spaces, participants learn to dream more boldly, and incorporate the details of a found space to help tell their stories.

CHAPTER 12

COMPOSITION TOWARD MAKING ORIGINAL WORK

There is a great appetite to work, and then
my sketchbook serves me as a cookbook
when I am hungry. I open it and even the
least of my sketches offers me material for
work.

—GEORGES BRAQUE

Composition exercises are especially helpful in the creation of
original work. The time set aside to generate Compositions
serves as an opportunity to sketch ideas in time and space, look
at them, respond to and critique them, and refine or define new
directions. Usually some of the material generated in the Compositional phase can be used directly in a production.

The following steps are meant to suggest a way to begin creating new work using Composition work as an aid to the investigation of a theme and the generation of new material.

STEP 1: THE BASIC BUILDING BLOCKS FOR DEVISED WORK

In the creation of original work, it is helpful for the process to be grounded in three basic components upon which a production can be constructed:

- The *question*
- The *anchor*
- The *structure*.

The *question* (or theme) motivates the entire process. This central driving force should be big enough, interesting enough and relevant enough to be attractive and contagious to many people. The *question* emerges from personal interest and then spreads like a virus to other people who come in contact with it.

The *anchor* is a person (or event) that can serve as a vehicle to get to the *question*.

The *structure* is the skeleton upon which the event hangs. It is a way to organize time, information, text and imagery.

Here are some examples of these three building blocks used in original productions by Anne and Tina:

1. *Culture of Desire* (a play devised by SITI Company about consumerism)

   - The *question*: Who are we becoming in light of the pervasive and rampant consumerism that permeates our every move through life?
   - The *anchor*: Andy Warhol.
   - The *structure*: Dante's *Inferno*.

2. *American Vaudeville* (a play written by Anne and Tina for Houston's Alley Theatre)

   - The *question*: What are the roots of American popular entertainment?

    □ The *anchor*: The actual testimonies and experiences of people who created and performed in vaudeville.
    □ The *structure*: A vaudeville show *structure*.

3. *Cabin Pressure* (a play by SITI Company, commissioned by the Humana Festival at Actors Theatre of Louisville)

    □ The *question*: What is the creative role of a theater audience?
    □ The *anchor*: A group of non-theater people are asked about their specific experiences encountering theater.
    □ The *structure*: An awkward audience "talkback" in a theater becomes a reverie and meditation.

STEP 2: GATHERING MATERIAL

Once the basic building blocks of the project are established, it is time to collect material that might be used in the production.

1. Make a list of everything that you know for sure about the project, including any ideas about character, text, situation, story, development, imagery, etc.
2. Make a list of everything that you do not know. What you do not know can be as useful as what you know. These gaps, these mysterious unknowns that make you uncertain and nervous about the piece, constitute fertile ground.
3. Collect text, imagery, music, sound, objects and whatever else feels "*Vice*" (see Chapter 10, page 124) in relation to the project. It is fine to bring too much to the table. You are simply pointing at things to help your collaborators into the Play-World. Everything you gather may become a clue or a vital component.

STEP 3: LATERAL THINKING

1. Share this accumulated information with your collaborators. It is important that the entire group becomes directly
   and personally involved right at the beginning of the
   rehearsal process. This sense of ownership will be palpable
   to an audience in the final production and can get your
   company through the dry spells of a long run. Invite them
   to find their *own* interest and to personalize the material.
   Ignite their passion. Sharing information can either occur
   in discussions around a table or in Composition assignments that are created by small work groups (see Source
   Work in the next chapter).

2. Present all the material you've gathered, and be ready to let
   any part of it go when necessary (see "Hold on tightly, let
   go lightly," page 161). Work in the spirit of trial and error.
   Be open to taking conceptual leaps of faith in order to allow
   for poetry and metaphor. Be open to new influences and
   points of view from other people. At the same time, try
   to stay in touch with the central question, the itch, your
   interest.

3. After all the collected materials and ideas have been shared,
   Lateral Thinking can begin. Lateral Thinking is a ground-
   breaking method of collaborative (in a group) dreaming
   (see Edward de Bono's book *Lateral Thinking: Creativity Step
   by Step*, Harper Perennial, New York, 1990). It is a nonjudg-
   mental process of collectively ruminating over solutions
   to particular shared problems. Freely associating off one
   another's ideas stimulates a collective image of the world of
   the play, and generates new and surprising ideas about
   what might happen within that arena.

   It is important for each and every participant to take
   ownership in the process. In putting your ideas out to the
   ensemble, you are opening your process to include them. In
   practicing Lateral Thinking, you are providing space for
   them to play and dream beside you. While you remain "the
   final word," the participants become your co-creators. They

are empowered. This is the time for them in which the project becomes less theoretical and more personal.

STEP 4: COMPOSITIONS

It is now time to devise your own Composition assignments for your particular project. The basic impulse behind the Compositional stage of rehearsal is the Brechtian: "Show me!" The objective of Composition work is to translate theory and ideas into action, event and image. It is an opportunity for the ensemble to explore the material in concrete, act*able* ways.

To create a Composition assignment, start with what *you* are wondering or confused about. Make a list of ideas and material you would like to explore. In giving the assignment, make sure that you are not describing results, but proposing puzzles that the group might solve.

Note: There is much overlap between the concepts and assignments suggested here and those in the next chapter (Composition Toward Rehearsing a Play). Feel free to browse and mix and match.

Each Composition assignment might explore one or more of the following qualities: point of view, architecture, the role of the audience, storytelling, light and color, character, etc.

Point of View

Whose *point of view* is at play? Whose story is it? How does the theme or subject change according to who tells it? Is the storyteller seen, embodied or implied? If the piece contains a question, who is asking the question? If it is a dream, who is the dreamer? If it is a memory or an exorcism or an argument, whose is it?

Architecture

How might you use the particular architecture of the theater and/or the set design? A Composition assignment might address and explore some novel ways to utilize the space. Perhaps the assignment asks the participants to break or fulfill the expectations that the architecture creates. How can you wake up the space in which the event will occur?

Role of Audience

What is the relationship of the actors to the audience? Should the audience feel like Peeping Toms, witness to something they should not see? Are they present at a public ceremony? Are they a jury at a trial? What is their role in the event? Compositions provide a way to explore various possibilities in determining a solution to this question.

Storytelling Techniques

What are the storytelling techniques that make your story come alive? The question here is not *what* you are telling, but *how*. The Composition might explore filmic techniques (montage) or Brechtian theatrical devices. Are you making transitions with blackouts or the ding of a bell or slow cross-fading techniques? Are these storytelling techniques consistent or do they transform during the course of the piece?

Genre

What is the genre? How can you employ forms from other sources? Is there a place for puppetry or ballet? What theatrical genres does this piece draw from? What historical devices might be useful? Is there a Greek chorus or a vaudeville sketch in the mix?

Framing Devices

What creates the borders, or edges, around the playing space—and how are these frames possibly used or shifted?

Scale

How might you use objects or actions that are very big or small?

Light and Color

How are light and color used to express the theme?

Language

What are the languages spoken? How do people communicate? Where does the text come from and how is it placed and spoken?

Character

What defines character in your work? Do characters emerge through action, description, music, etc.?

Play-World

What is the arena, the landscape or the world of the play? (See the discussion of Play-World in the next chapter.)

STEP 5: ASSIGN AND CREATE

Divide the ensemble into small work groups and have each group tackle the same assignment. Allow a minimum of an hour and a maximum of a few days for the groups to rehearse and stage their Compositions. Encourage the groups to work on their feet during at least sixty percent of the allotted time (too much discussion stymies the results). Encourage everyone to create intuitively and without fear of failure. The best Compositions are often a combination of failures and giant leaps.

STEP 6: PRESENT AND DISCUSS

Perform all the Compositions, one after the next, with no commentary in between. Welcome the work with openness and generosity. Encourage the participants to take time in the performances to really meet one another onstage, rather than just mechanically moving from image to image, idea to idea. As Peter Brook described in *The Empty Space* (Touchstone, New York, 1996), a stage space has two rules: (1) Anything *can* happen and (2) Something *must* happen. It is the performers' responsibility to make sure that something actually occurs between them when they present their Composition.

Give feedback for each Composition by focusing on the positive innovations. Articulate what is useful to the production. Recognize any risks that were incurred, and support the effort. List the pitfalls that came up and welcome discoveries of what to avoid while putting together the production at hand. Allow for individual reactions to the Compositions. Listen to all responses as clues to solving a great mystery.

Here are some phrases that we have found useful in discussing the process of Composition work:

A universe from scratch.

Making original work offers the opportunity to create *a universe from scratch*. You can, in fact, create a universe with its own laws of time, space and logic. It is certainly possible to do this by studying and replicating an actual time and place if that is what the piece requires, but you also have the ability to say: "Anything is possible. So what should happen?" or "Why should objects fall to the ground as opposed to float upward?" With a healthy sense of adventure and facing a blank page, you set off into the unknown. (See Play-World section in the next chapter.)

Hold on tightly, let go lightly.

Dive into any endeavor with strength, fortitude and intention, but at the same time be willing to adjust. Know what you want, and be completely unattached to getting it.

Leap of faith.

Without an intuitive *leap of faith,* work remains academic. Have the courage to make choices that you cannot justify at the time. These choices constitute a leap.

> Living is a form of not being sure, not knowing what is next or how. The moment you know how, you begin to die a little. The artist never entirely knows, we guess. We may be wrong, but we take leap after leap in the dark.
>
> —AGNES DE MILLE

> It is supposed to be the most difficult feat for a ballet dancer to leap into a specific posture in such a way that he never once strains for the posture but in the very leap assumes the posture . . . Most people live completely absorbed in worldly joys and sorrows; they are benchwarmers who do not take part in the dance. The knights of infinity are ballet dancers and have elevation. They make the upward movement . . .
>
> —SØREN KIERKEGAARD, *FEAR AND TREMBLING*

CHAPTER 13

COMPOSITION TOWARD REHEARSING A PLAY

SOURCE WORK

In creating new work, you work from a *source*, whether it is a question, an image, a historical event, etc. In working on a play, you also encounter a source. The play becomes your source, and it, in itself, contains others.

Source Work is a series of activities done at the beginning of the rehearsal process to get in touch (both intellectually and emotionally, both individually and collectively) with the source from which you are working. It's the time taken (before you begin rehearsing anything the audience might actually witness onstage) to enter with your entire being into the world, the issues, the heart of your material. Source Work can include, but is not limited to the work done in Viewpoints and Composition training.

Source Work can take many forms. It may include presentations or reports given by actors on specified topics, learning period dances, building a group art installation and, of course, Composition. Source Work can be anything your imagination devises, as long as it moves the company closer to the material and an investment in it.

Source Work allows for silent and invisible communication. Source Work is a way of lighting the fire so that everyone can share in it. It's not about staging. It's not about setting the final product. It's about making time at the beginning of the process (sometimes only a day or two, sometimes a month or more, depending always on time limitations) to wake up the *question* inside the piece in a true, personal way for everyone involved.

Source Work asks the entire company to participate with its entire being in the process, rather than assume a prescribed or passive role. It asks each person to contribute, create and care, rather than wait to be told what the play is about or what their blocking should be.

A director often does Source Work on her/his own before rehearsals begin. Anne reads a ton of books and listens to dozens of new CDs. Tina cuts out photographs and sticks them all over her walls. Other directors might go to the library, make field trips, talk to people, conduct any kind of research or preparation that may inform the work. So when a director walks into rehearsal on the first day, s/he is often weeks or months ahead of the rest of the company in her/his obsession with the material. Source Work is used to provide a time and space for *all* the collaborators to fill up with their own knowledge, interest, dreams and reactions to the material. Think of it this way: the director has caught a disease, and somehow in these critical early moments of the process, s/he has to make the disease contagious. Source Work spreads the disease. *Source Work is an invitation to obsession.*

The source is anything that is the origin for the work at hand. Source Work is about getting in touch with this original impulse *behind* the work, as well as the work itself, i.e., the text, its relevance, its period, its author, or the physical and aural world of the production. The source of a theater piece can be as intangible as a feeling or as concrete as a newspaper clipping or found object. Theater can be made with anything as its source.

Source Work is the time we put aside to *riff* off the source, to respond to it as a group, and to cause and identify an explosive chemistry between it and us.

Source Work in Rehearsal

The customary research and discussion that often begins a rehearsal process could be considered a form of Source Work. These useful activities ask the company to work from their heads. They include:

- Watching related movies, videos, DVDs
- Listening to related music
- Reporting on related topics, including historical research on the movement, etiquette, etc., of the period of the piece.

Building on this preliminary "head work," Source Work is designed to awaken the intuition but also the *un*conscious.

When introducing Source Work to a company of actors, let them know that *you* know what you are asking them to do: to make choices and declarations *way too early and fast*. This is purposeful. Their choices are meant to erupt out of instinct. And the choices can (and will) change tomorrow.

Actors might initially feel that Source Work is either "a waste of time" (another silly theater game) or a misuse of valuable time that could be spent doing table work or scene work. The reality is: Source Work saves time. Time spent up front in the rehearsal process getting the company on the same page is time saved later from having to explain over and over again what that "page" is. Coming to an agreement about goals and developing a shared vocabulary saves time later, as everyone moves into staging, run-throughs, tech, previews, opening.

Source Work Rehearsal Example 1: *Katchen von Heilbronn*

At the first rehearsal for Heinrich von Kleist's play *Katchen von Heilbronn*, which Anne directed at American Repertory Theatre's Institute for Advanced Theatre Training, Anne asked everyone to come in on the second day with a list or presentation that answered the question: "What is German?" She was not interested in academic research that would bring the actors to the material from their heads, but in subjective responses that would bring them to the material from their imaginations, preconceptions, prejudices, fantasies, memories, histories and culture. She wanted to bring their hidden selves to the surface through Source Work. So when they came in on the second day of rehearsal, one person read a list of things German, another brought in German food, and Tina played the most clichéd German music she could think of on the piano, ranging from Beethoven's Fifth Symphony to the Nazi anthem "Tomorrow Belongs to Me" from *Cabaret*. In this way, they were able to identify where they, as a group, were in relationship to the *German-ness* of the play, become aware of its context, and decide how to operate out of that (or not). In this way, a forgotten culture becomes and active culture.

Source Work Rehearsal Example 2: *Strindberg Sonata*

When Tina visited Anne in rehearsal for *Strindberg Sonata* (a piece she made about August Strindberg's world at the University of California at San Diego), Anne was in the middle of Source Work with the company. She had asked the actors to fill in the blanks: "When I think of Strindberg, I see _____, I hear _____, I smell _____," etc. On the day Tina visited they were reading their lists out loud. They were full of images of men in top hats and women in long gowns of crimson and black velvet, Edvard Munch paintings, the sound of a piano playing, a clock ticking, a gunshot, the smell of paper burning, liquor on someone's breath, a bouquet of flowers, etc. The first things that came up were often the most obvious, but Anne encouraged the actors to lean into the clichés and stereotypes rather than try to ignore them. By going through them, she explained, they would come out on the other side with something that *used*, but transformed, them. More importantly, the lists served to awaken the imaginations of the actors, and help create the vocabulary for their Play-World.

THE PLAY-WORLD

When directing a piece, start with the assumption that you can create an entirely new universe onstage: a Play-World (see previous chapter, "a universe from scratch"). Rather than take for granted that the reality of the play will be the same as our everyday reality, work with an attitude that anything in this Play-World can be *invented from scratch*. The Play-World is the set of laws belonging to your piece and no other: the way time operates, the way people dress, the color palette, what constitutes good or evil, good manners or bad, what a certain gesture denotes, etc. Use Source Work to create the Play-World of any given piece. Out of tasks (like the two rehearsal examples provided above), develop a list that defines this new world. Sometimes these lists are concrete and historical (as in the way people held cigarettes in turn-of-the-century Russia, so as to make them last longer), sometimes they are invented (in Anne's SITI production of *Small Lives/Big Dreams*, a distillation of Chekhov's five major plays, everyone had to enter from stage right and exit stage left, so that to exit stage right took on a specific meaning of breaking the rules, leaving the game, going backward, going toward death). A society in India is different than a society in France— how exactly? What do these differences *look like*, how do you make them active onstage? French society in 1800 is different from French society in 1850—how exactly?

Every culture has its own rules, spoken or not, as does every household, every relationship, every landscape. Even theater has its performative rules: face the audience, stand in the light, pause for a laugh. Why? Says who?

Find a compelling reason to make a piece where everyone has their backs to the audience except when they tell a secret or tell a lie—only in those moments do they face front. What would this express to an audience?

Assume nothing. *Question* everything. Invent the rules. Make a unique Play-World.

Compositions Toward a Play

In rehearsal, by taking time to do Composition work toward a production, we generate material:

- That can be used in performance
- That can be a jumping-off point for discussion and example
- That is quick and dirty, extreme and spontaneous and, therefore, often reveals enormous and deep truths about the play that might be forgotten or never explored.

You can create Composition assignments that focus on:

- Themes of the play
- The physical world of the play
- A character in the play
- A relationship in the play
- A scene or event in the play.

EXERCISE 1: BASIC THEME COMPOSITION

Divide the cast into groups. Ask each group to decide, among themselves, and only for today, "what the play is about." Make a three-minute Composition that distills the essence of the play and expresses its theme according to the group. The assignment can be given without any other ingredients, or may include as many as you think useful.

EXERCISE 2: ADVANCED THEME COMPOSITION

1. Divide the cast into groups.
2. Articulate a theme of the play that interests you. (Provide this for the company, or ask each group to choose their own.)
3. Divide the play into three main movements (some plays clearly have three movements, others two, others five). Name and define these for the groups, or let each group determine their own breakdown.
4. Create a piece in three parts (corresponding to the parts of the play) that expresses the thematic core of the material. The sections can either flow one into the next, or have a separating device for each (a title card, a blackout, the ringing of a bell, a voice-over). In either case, each of the three parts should have a clear beginning, middle and end, so there is no confusion about when one part concludes and another begins.
5. Incorporate the following elements one at a time:

   - Three lines of text from the play text (no more, no less)
   - A specific role for the audience, and choice of performing space in relation to viewing space
   - A piece of music from an unexpected source
   - A revelation of space
   - A surprise entrance
   - A break of frame
   - A sequence of extreme contrast
   - A repetition of an object or image three times
   - Anything else from your specific list of ingredients, from your specific Play-World.

EXERCISE 3: COMPOSITION ON THE PHYSICAL/AURAL WORLD OF THE PLAY

This assignment should be given the night before the next rehearsal, so that the company has just enough time (but not too much) to scavenge for stuff.

1. Divide the cast into trios, pairs or have people work alone.

2. Using only found objects and sounds (no actors), have them create a two-minute piece that expresses the physical and aural world of your play. No person can appear in the piece, except, if necessary, a technical manipulator, a kind of puppeteer for the landscape. Create something expressive and subjective, rather than representational. Not: "What does our set look like?" But: "What does the environment of our Play-World *feel* like?" Is it chaotic or formal or pinched or romantic? How do you create this feeling through found objects and sounds?

3. Choose a space that is controlled and focused, so that there are no accidents in terms of light leakage or ambient sounds from outside.

4. Elements to consider and work with include:

   ◻ PLACE. Where does the piece take place? Not literally, but expressively. Is it a battlefield, a temple, a no-man's-land, a circus, the inside of someone's head, a particular character's dream?

   ◻ TIME. When does the piece take place? One might approach this literally and create, for instance, a portrait of the Gilded Age. Or one might approach it more subjectively, and focus on the Gilded Age as remembered by someone particular; or the way that the events in the play are all repetitions of each other, and therefore time is circular; or the notion that the entire play feels cloaked in a never-ending night.

   ◻ MATERIALS AND TEXTURES. Color, weight, durability. Is the landscape all lush velvets, or is it all rusty nails with a sliver of torn velvet in the center?

   ◻ IMAGES AND OBJECTS. Size, shape, color. Is it a collage made of hundreds of magazine cutouts, or a field of five-foot-long stemmed roses, or a single tiny glittering object in an empty space? Is it a rose in a vase, or a rose next to a revolver?

□ POINT OF VIEW. Perspective, scale. Is the piece being remembered or dreamed or told by anyone in particular? What is her taste, her opinion, her intention? Who is the audience? Do we look from outside the Play-World or are we immersed in it? Do we see things from above or below or in close-up?

□ SOUND. Music, text, sound effects, recorded or live? Is there silence or a lot of noise? Is the noise quiet or loud? Is there text? What sounds create the atmosphere? Is it a long, melancholy cello solo, or a long, melancholy cello solo punctuated by bursts of suppressed giggling?

□ LIGHT. Intensity, direction, color, quality of air. Are things clear and luminous or mysterious and hidden in shadow? Is the environment natural or man-made? Is it a flashlight searching through smoke or ten candles on the floor or a floodlight through a door directed at the audience? Does light change imperceptibly or in sharp bumps?

□ PROGRESSION. Does the physical landscape change in the course of the action? How? Is it slowly getting brighter over the course of two minutes, or does a ball roll onstage in the last ten seconds, knocking everything over?

EXERCISE 4: CHARACTER COMPOSITION

1. Choose a character that interests you today. (You could also give the more conventional assignment of having each actor work on the character s/he is actually playing.)
2. Create a character study in five portraits, each portrait separated by a blackout of no more than ten seconds. Hold each portrait at least twenty seconds so it can be studied.
3. Each portrait of the character must include:

□ One object

□ One piece of music or external sound.

4. The titles of the five portraits are as follows:

□ *The fear of* . . . (must express something about what the character is most afraid of)

□ *Love or hatred of* . . . (choose one; must identify a person or thing the character most loves or hates)

□ *Fantasies of* . . . (must portray what the character fantasizes about and/or how)

□ *Memories of* . . . (must address what the character remembers)

□ *The desire for* . . . (must express something about what the character most wants, longs for, is propelled by).

EXERCISE 5: RELATIONSHIP COMPOSITION

Part 1: Essence of Relationship

1. Divide the cast into couples.
2. Each couple has two minutes to make a movement sequence that expresses the essence of their relationship through the use of Spatial Relationship, Tempo, Gesture, Topography and any other individual Viewpoints that come into play.

Part 2: Progression of Relationship

1. Divide the cast into couples.
2. Each couple has two minutes to make a movement sequence that tells the story of the progression of their relationship through the course of the play through the use of Spatial Relationship, Tempo, Gesture, Topography and any other individual Viewpoints that come into play.

EXERCISE 6: EVENT COMPOSITION

1. Choose a problematic or perplexing scene in the play.
2. Divide into groups.
3. Each group should break the scene down into three to eight sections or mini-chapters. Give each one a label, indicating the fundamental action of that section.
4. Following the outline of the determined mini-chapters (rather than the lines of text in the scene), translate the action of each mini-chapter into expressive movement.
5. Present, discuss, point to (as in, "If you can't say it, point to it," a method of simply identifying what belongs, works or sticks through example).

CHAPTER 14

COMPOSITION AS PRACTICE AND ADDITIONAL RECIPES

A ballet dancer practices by doing exercises at the bar. A pianist practices by playing scales. A basketball player shoots hoops, while another lifts weights or jogs. How do we, as makers of theater, keep in shape? How do we work out? Viewpoints can be practice for the participants as they exercise the muscles of *openness*, *awareness* and *spontaneity*. Similarly, Composition can be practice for directors, choreographers, playwrights, composers, designers, performers—all creators of theater. In Composition work, we practice *creating*. We keep in shape our ability to be *bold*, *articulate*, *playful* and *expressive*.

Just as Viewpoints training is designed to help performers get out of their heads, so is Composition work designed to help directors, et al., get out of their heads. Composition work does not have to be used only in a production or in making original pieces; it can be used in class, workshop or anytime a group of people want to get together to *work out*. Through Composition work, we learn to trust our instincts, to refine what we make, to recognize our strengths and weaknesses as artists and, above all, we learn secrets about ourselves through what emerges.

In various cities in which we have worked, there are now ad hoc groups that meet to simply practice Viewpoints and make Composition pieces together. In New York, Chicago and Los Angeles, these groups gather and turn on some music and begin Viewpointing. Or they choose a subject and generate material through Compositions. They have no opening night, no critics, no end in mind—only to practice, to keep their creative spirits active and flexible.

> The word "composition" moved me spiritu-
> ally, and I later made it my aim in life to paint
> a "composition." It affected me like a prayer
> and filled me with awe.
>
> —WASSILY KANDINSKY

PRACTICE EXERCISES

You can practice or explore *anything* in your Composition work. You can do Composition exercises on your own, with one other person, or in larger groups. You can do them anywhere, with a lot of stuff or nothing at all. The subject, the focus, the goal, the ingredients—they are all yours to choose. Anything is possible and the sky is the limit.

PRACTICE EXERCISE 1: OBSERVATION AND ARTICULATION

1. Choose three sources that affect you or interest you. Your source can be an image (photo, postcard, Xerox), a story, a newspaper clipping, a song, an object, etc. Don't worry about whether or not you can or know how to make a piece from this source, just begin with what moves you.

2. For all three:

  □ Describe how the source affects you—your intu-
    itive response to it. ("It makes me feel sad," etc.)
  □ Deconstruct *why* it affects you. Analyze the
    Compositional elements at work. Try to articulate
    how *form* creates *feeling* in each particular case. Is it
    the scale that moves you or the opposition of lines
    or the associative links you have with a specific
    icon? In deconstructing your source, pay attention
    to size, texture, shape, color, tempo, rhythm, repe-
    tition, contrast (light and dark, fast and slow, etc.).

PRACTICE EXERCISE 2: LANDSCAPE AND TOPOGRAPHY

1. Work together in groups of two. One person will invent the
   landscape, the other will present it by traveling through it.
2. The couples work in an empty space. The Landscape
   Architect from each couple mentally divides the space into
   discrete sections, including specific sizes and shapes (s/he
   might work with quadrants, lanes, pathways, etc.), and
   assigns a physical quality or law to each area. For instance,
   one corner might require an extremely fast tempo, another
   might have a reversed gravity where things go up instead of
   down, another might cause everything to go backward,
   another might demand a slithering on the floor through an
   imaginary crevice.
3. Once a complex, detailed, specific *invisible landscape* has
   been created and experienced by the person moving through
   it, each couple should present this to the group. The terrain
   should be clearly legible.

PRACTICE EXERCISE 3: COLOR

1. Have small groups Viewpoint off colors in the room, while
   the rest of the group observes.

2. Or, have each group choose three objects, each with a distinct color. Using these three objects, create a story, that grows out of the three colors and how they interact.

3. Or, individually name a color and list all associations you have with it. What feeling does it engender in you, what does it remind you of, what characters does it make you think of, what are its traditional symbolic references? Go through many colors. Design a Composition that explores a controlled, conscious color choice. For instance, you could do "a purple piece," or a piece in three sections titled: "White," "Red," "Black," or a piece in which characters are defined and interact based on the color of a single object they wear.

EXERCISE 1: STAGE YOUR FAMILY AT DINNER

1. This exercise can be done with one or more groups.

2. One person in each group directs the others in a staging of her/his own family at dinner. The staging should be "Expressive," meaning that it should be less a literal depiction of the characters and events than an expression of the subjective experience of what it felt like to be there, in the midst of that family. Each director casts individuals to play siblings and parents, etc. The director must also choose someone to play her/himself. The dinner can be from any time in the family's history.

3. One at a time, each group shows its Composition to the others.

4. The director should give each individual a personal note, and give the group one general note that will help make their performances even more expressive of the dynamics of the family. The Composition should then be performed again.

In an exercise like this one, staging your family at dinner, you know the feeling, the individuals and the event intimately. The dramaturgy is distinct and particular. When working on a play you should strive for this same intimacy, the same *working-from-feel*. This entails a great deal of study, imagination and personalization.

EXERCISE 2: COMPOSITIONS BASED ON ARTHUR MILLER'S *DEATH OF A SALESMAN*

1. EXPRESSING CHARACTER. Choose a character from Arthur Miller's *Death of a Salesman*, and a moment in the play in which this character speaks. Stage the same moment in five different ways with the same actor.
2. EXPRESSING RELATIONSHIP. Choose two characters from Arthur Miller's *Death of a Salesman*, and a specific interaction they share in the play. Stage the same interaction in five different ways with the same two actors.
3. POINT OF VIEW and DREAM LOGIC. Stage Arthur Miller's *Death of a Salesman* as a dream or nightmare of one of the characters. Use as many actors as necessary. The event should be a maximum of ten minutes.

These Compositions offer the chance to apply the principles of Viewpoints training directly to character and relationships in a play. Suggested possibilities to express character and relationship: physical action, distance from or closeness to the audience, distance from or closeness to one another, Tempo of speech, Tempo of movement, use of Architecture, Gesture, Shape, Dynamic (loudness or softness), Pitch, etc.

EXERCISE 3: CLASSICAL PLAYS AS THE SOURCE FOR COMPOSITIONS

In small groups (usually between two to six):

1. DECONSTRUCTION. Choose a classic play. Do the entire play in ten minutes.
2. LINE. Choose a scene from a classic play. Do the scene with concentration on the line, *the pull*, so that there is an

unbroken line of dramatic action moving forward (that *pulls* the audience forward) with no snags or detours.

3. INTERRUPTIONS. Choose a scene from a classic play. Do the scene with fifteen interruptions.

EXERCISE 4: RADIO PLAY

1. In groups of three to eight, create an eight-minute Composition in the form of a radio play. The purpose of the exercise is to create a journey for the audience through sound.

2. Depending on whether you are doing this Composition toward a production or for practice, you can assign the Composition to be built around a particular scene, a theme, a story, etc.

3. Decide which ingredients to include, using any of the elements or devices from the other Compositions, such as broken expectation, surprise entrance, fifteen consecutive seconds of silence, a slap, etc.

4. Give a half hour for the groups to prepare their Compositions, and then perform them one at a time, with the audience keeping their eyes closed throughout.

CHAPTER 15

HOW TO DISCUSS COMPOSITION WORK IN A GROUP

After performing some Composition work, have the entire group sit together. Ask everyone to close their eyes. Talk to the group about each Composition performed that day, one at a time, and ask people what they remember. This process of remembering should not be an intellectual or analytical exercise, rather, each individual should relax and focus on her/his memory of each Composition to see what *floats up* into consciousness. Then ask everyone to state aloud what has *stayed* with them (not what they liked and disliked). People should keep their eyes closed and listen so that they can hear each other; individuals should speak clearly and loudly and try not to overlap each other. What *floats up* will be what drew genuine, unmediated interest. You might hear: "The way Agnes touched the flower" or "When the balloon was released." The focus should remain on a concrete account of events and images, rather than their effect or interpretation.

This time of reflection represents a fundamental tool in creating work for the stage. Although analytical criticism and theoretical discussion will play a significant role in the feedback, one's own body and memory can be the most meaningful barometer in the artistic process. Recall a production or concert or painting or piece of music that you encountered three or four years ago. What do you remember about it? Quite often what you remember indicates what you must look for in your own work. What stays with you might be considered the most successful aspect of the event. The same is true for a rehearsal. What *floats up* before you go to sleep at night after a day of rehearsal? Quite often what stays with you was not actually planned but, rather, happened by accident. And yet these accidents are signals to which we should pay attention. Ultimately, as Sigmund Freud taught us, there is no such thing as an accident. In this case, it is a gift.

Ask the participants to open their eyes. Now as a group revisit each Composition, one at a time, closely analyzing the work. Look in detail at the moments that were described as memorable. What made the choices theatrical? Try to recognize and examine the building blocks of those *memorable moments*. Give verbal notes on all aspects of every Composition and allow participants to contribute their own thoughts and reactions. If you are working toward a production and the Compositions have been explorations toward staging, now is the time to comment on what was "*Vice*" or "not *Vice*" (see Chapter 10, page 124). If it is a class, now is the opportunity to analyze the language of theater and discuss the point-of-view, the audience's journey and how the particular actors embodied the moments and met one another onstage.

Here are some things to watch for in Composition work, which may be utilized in the discussion:

- How did the given ingredients (the list of what must be included in the Composition) affect the experience of watching? For example, if *a broken expectation* was one of the ingredients, how did the *broken expectation* shape the audience's experience?
- How did the collaboration go? Were there any moments where the process shut down? Were there any moments of ease and flow? Why?

- As an audience, what did you find exciting in the event? What happened that made the pulse race faster? Why?
- What did you pay attention to? Why?
- When did you space-out and not feel part of the event? Why?
- Did you empathize with anyone in the Composition? What made that happen?
- How was character created? Were you able to identify characters and keep track of them? How?
- Which parts of the Composition were Descriptive and which were Expressive? (See Chapter 11, page 146.)
- Were there any moments of pure stage poetry? At what moment does the language of the stage become poetic?
- How was the jo-ha-kyu of the whole event, and how did jo-ha-kyu function within the parts of the Composition? (See Chapter 11, page 147.)
- How were transitions handled?
- What expectations did the opening moments of the Composition create and how were those expectations handled?
- Was the ending clear and necessary?
- Was a strong and active choice made about space, setting and architecture?
- Was there a clear role for the audience in this Composition, and was it supported by the way they entered, sat or moved?
- Could you feel the impulse behind the work? Was there a *question* that had to be asked or a statement that needed to be made? Could you feel necessity in the piece?
- How was text used, and was there awkwardness or ease in the moments when people spoke? Was there a place for the spoken word? What made speaking necessary?
- How articulate was the physicality in the Composition?
- Were repetition and recycling used in an expressive way?
- How were individual Viewpoints apparent in the Composition?
- What were the strengths of the piece and what were its weaknesses? Was it strong in character, story, atmosphere, imagery, language or theme? And which of those elements were weakest?

- How vivid were the sound choices, including music, silence and aural landscape?
- Did the Composition find articulate ways to work with available light, whether sunlight in the room, overhead fluorescent or found lighting (such as flashlights, clip-lights, candlelight, theatrical lighting, etc.)?
- Can the Composition be discussed in terms of other art forms? Were there moments or devices that parallel film language, such as close-up, establishing shot, montage, etc.? Or painting, such as framing, size of canvas, how many colors were in the palate? Or music, such as tempo, crescendo, pitch, codas etc.?
- Was the length of the piece itself expressive? Was it long enough but not too long to accomplish what it needed to?
- Did the audience know where to look and did that matter?
- Was there conflict in the piece and does that matter? Was there tension and suspense in the piece and does that matter?
- Was there humor and does that matter? Why? What makes something funny?
- Was there a sense from the audience of being firmly in someone's hands. Did they feel taken care of and guided?

Tesseracts.

Madeline L'Engle invented the term *tesseract* in her book *A Wrinkle in Time* (Bantam Doubleday Dell, New York, 1962). In the book she describes the image of a piece of string that someone is holding with one end in each hand. One end of the string is described as Point A and the other end is Point B. We traditionally believe that to travel from Point A to Point B we must travel the length of the string, horizontally. In a *tesseract*, it's as if we take the two ends of the string and put them together at the exact same time and place so that the length of the string collapses into a vertical, and in this case, invisible time and place. So what happens in a *tesseract* is that we instantaneously travel from one state to another without transition. This can happen in *time*—for example, it's winter and in the blink of an eye it's spring. It can happen in *place*—for example, in describing a dream, we might say: ". . . and suddenly I was in an open field." It can happen in the theater, in acting, in a way that Ms. L'Engle probably never imagined—for example, a character doesn't become progressively more angry, s/he *tesseracts* from a state of absolute calm to a state of absolute rage, *without transition*. In human psychology (and in studying a text), we are taught that a person goes from A to B to C to D. But, if a character *tesseracts* onstage, they might go from A to G, then back to B and suddenly to X. Once we open our eyes to the possibility of *tesseracts*, we begin to notice that, in fact, it is not just a fanciful notion, but also an accurate description of the way people behave all around us all the time.

Shortly before German playwright Heiner Müller died, he visited Columbia University to speak with graduate theater students. After a long, brilliant, eloquent, complex talk, a bright-eyed young student raised his hand with the question: "Mr. Müller, do you have any advice for a young actor?" There was a moment of silence. "Yes," replied Müller generously, "because you have a body, you do not need transitions."

This advice could require a lifetime to understand and digest, but at the same time it helps to crystallize the notion that we don't *always* have to think our way from one state to another. So often we want to understand why a character goes from A to G, but we discover that in simply going from A to G, in simply putting it in our bodies, in simply *doing* it, there is a kind of understanding that emerges, an understanding beyond reason and psychology. Sometimes, without reason or conscious motivation, we simply *transition* from one extreme state to another. This is human. This is natural.

Tesseracts can also be applied to playwriting. For example, the playwright Chuck Mee has said that he sometimes conceives of his characters "as being like beautiful long-stemmed wine glasses that have been thrown to the ground and shattered into a million pieces." Rather than putting them back together into an expected coherence, Mee glues mismatching shards in unexpected ways, creating a new form out of old fragments. Instead of the expected psychological arc of a character moving from A to B to C, Mee's characters often start in C, then abruptly switch gears into F or J or X, without the traditional psychological signposts to guide them (and us). (For further review of Chuck Mee's work, see charlesmee.org.)

The same, only different.

Composition is a form of writing, but it is writing on your feet in space and time using the language of the theater. Just as there are literary devices in fiction and poetry, there are useful theatrical devices in making Compositions. Think of small stage moments— a gesture, a turn, a light cue—as words. In combining these *words*, you begin to create sentences. And in stringing these sentences together, you begin to build a paragraph, and so on, into chapters, etc., all with a combination of movement, light, sound, etc.

In literature we are familiar with devices such as allusion and onomatopoeia. These are tools that allow for a greater range of expression. Here we introduce a useful *theatrical equivalent*, which we call *the same, only different*. Repetition is a basic building block in both Viewpoints and Composition. The writer Gertrude Stein taught us that with a small vocabulary of words, much can be expressed. When something is repeated, it is never really the same and contains within it the memory of the last time it was seen or heard. We call this *the same, only different*. This concept is useful and can be found in music (the repetition of melodies or lines), architecture (the repetition of shapes or volumes), painting, etc. By setting up a pattern of repetition, we can draw attention to what breaks the pattern and is therefore different, or what changes.

For example, if you want a group of people to appear to the audience as unique individuals onstage, you can highlight their differences by having them all do the same thing. If they all do something different, you will only see what they *do*. If they all do the *same* thing, you will see the differences between them—you will see who they *are*.

An example: a Composition begins with a woman sitting alone at a bare table. In the course of the Composition, the woman goes on a journey of some kind. The piece ends with the woman again sitting at the table. However, this time there is a vase with a red rose on the table. The presence of the rose now becomes the focus or the essence of the final image, because everything else remains the same; it alone is different. If other things in the image were to change, for example, the table is different, the woman is sitting in a new position, etc., the rose would not be as eloquent.

Tracks.

A complete theater moment is comprised of separate tracks. Just as in film where there is a sound track and a visual track, in the theater there is a movement track, a text track, a lighting track, a sound track, a time track, and so on. The meaning of the piece emerges through the interrelationship of these various tracks. Do they agree or disagree? Do they complement each other or contradict each other?

The Swiss playwright Friedrich Durrenmatt insisted that the theater begins with a disagreement between what one sees and what one hears. "If I go to the theater," he wrote, "and I close my eyes, and I understand what I am hearing, then it is not theater, it is a lecture. If I go to the theater and close my ears, and I understand what I am seeing, then it is not theater, it's a slide show. The theater begins with a disagreement between what you see and what you hear."

How many times have you gone to the theater and watched people rotate around a couch for two hours, illustrating what they say with what they do? Compare this behavior with that of real life where people rarely do what they say. It is a rare moment when one person faces another and says: "I love you." Usually the words are uttered as someone is leaving the room looking at his watch. This difference between what is seen and what is heard expresses a basic truth about the relationship portrayed.

If the tracks all do the same thing, they cancel each other out.

Robert Wilson often uses the image of a candelabra atop a grand piano. Because both these objects seemingly belong together, come from the same world, we look at them with a sense of ease and familiarity. The relatedness of the objects doesn't challenge us to perceive what is distinct about each one. Wilson suggests that if you remove the candelabra and put in its place a Coke bottle, the contrast of the objects and what they evoke wake the image up. The image becomes a *strange attractor*.

In the film *Platoon*, the director Oliver Stone chose to present his famous battle sequence not with the expected accompanying sounds of violence and warfare, bombs going off and cries of anguish, but against Samuel Barber's excruciatingly beautiful and meditative "Adagio for Strings." In addition to setting violence against serene music, he worked with an extreme contrast of duration by juxtaposing the sustained musical arc with shorter edited shots. As the music climbed higher and higher, the imagery sank deeper and deeper into the mud. This disjunction between what was seen and what was heard accelerated during the course of the scene. Stone's capacity to express both horror and beauty in the same moment is what distinguishes his vision and makes the sequence remarkable.

Another example of the use of multiple contrasting tracks appears in the plays of Anton Chekhov. Every time Chekhov writes in a stage direction: "laughing through tears," he is drawing a contrast between what the character is feeling and what they are doing. At the end of *Uncle Vanya* when Sonya says: "Work, we must work," her verbal and physical action is disparate from her interior emotional life. Although she is experiencing grief and loss she is not crying but stating her resolve. In this way Chekhov taps into a universal and pervasive truth about human nature—what we feel and what we do are rarely the same.

CHAPTER 16

COMPOSITION AND RELATED ARTS

Composition work draws on all the arts, because to study and learn from *all* the arts is to enrich your output as an artist. In this chapter, we offer some devices or principles from related arts fields that can be especially useful in making Compositions.

Watch, read, listen and study: novels, essays, movies, paintings, concerts. What do you see and hear and experience that can be applied to your work in making theater?

We have not provided answers here, only questions. To illustrate, we offer a simple example, in this case from film:

How do you stage the theatrical equivalent of a *close-up*? Possibilities include:

- Everything is black except for a single pin spot on one hand.
- A person is dressed in all red except for a single white glove on one hand.
- The entire stage is motionless except for one person's hand, which is gently tapping.

◻ A group of people rush to the downstage edge, freezing in a very exact position, except for the person at center who continues movement by only turning her/his head very slowly.

MUSIC

METER. Is your piece in 3/4 or 4/4 or 6/8 time? What are the differences between these? Is your piece more of a waltz or a march? How do you manifest this?

TEMPO. Is your piece fast or slow? How do tempos change? What is adagio, largo, presto, etc.? How do you incorporate these notions of time into your work?

TONALITY (AND ATONALITY)/KEY. Is your piece major or minor? Is it tonal or atonal? Are the chords harmonious or dissonant? And what do these mean in terms of staging?

COUNTERPOINT. How many staves are in your Composition? How many voices work in counterpoint at once? Is it a smooth obbligato in contrast to a choppy underbelly, or what?

STRUCTURE. What is the *structure* of a fugue, a symphony, an étude, a nocturne, etc.? Which is your piece most like?

CODA. How do you make use of the notion of a coda? What purpose does it serve? What emotional satisfaction does it provide? What would a coda for your piece be? Is it worth playing with one?

REPEATS. As in music, when there are double lines indicating a return to previous material, does your Composition include repetition over time—going back and covering the same measures again? Why?

MUSICAL DIRECTIVE. How much are you aware of your piece as music? Can you use terms such as crescendo, decrescendo, pianissimo, accelerando, etc., to help shape your material?

ORCHESTRATION. How is your work orchestrated? How many instruments are you using to express the material? Would you say your palette is more woodwind than brass, more percussion, more strings? How is this translated into theatrical language?

PAINTING

SCHOOLS. If your Composition were from a school of painting, which one would it be?—Impressionism, expressionism, abstractionism, minimalism? Is it a landscape or figure, pastoral or portrait?

FRAMING. What is the frame of your piece? Is it framed at all? What else can be a frame other than a proscenium? What does it mean to *break the frame*?

SIZE OF CANVAS. How big is the canvas upon which you are working? Is it epic in scale or is it a miniature?

MEDIUM. How can you apply the notion of different mediums to your work in the theater? Stage a piece that is a watercolor, as opposed to an oil painting or collage. What qualities does a watercolor possess? What are the stage equivalents of these qualities?

COLOR. What colors are you painting with? How many? Do they compliment each other or clash?

PERSPECTIVE. What perspective are you using for the "eye" of the viewer? Look at various paintings. Compare their varied and extreme use of perspective (from below, zoomed in, etc.) to that of theater productions you've seen.

SCALE. How big are the objects and/or figures within the frame?

LINE. Note how your favorite paintings can be reduced to a skeleton of intersecting lines and shapes. When you paint onstage, how do you use strong lines: diagonals, dissections, curves, etc.?

COMPOSITION. How is your stage like a canvas inside a frame, and where are objects/figures placed within the canvas to create strong Composition? What is strong Composition? How can the separate elements be rearranged to create a new meaning or feeling?

LIGHT AND SHADOW. How do painters use light and shadow? Look at Vermeer, Bonnard, De Chirico, Wyeth, Hockney, Warhol. How do you paint with light onstage?

PRESENTATION. What are the various ways in which paintings are presented? What is the difference in going to a gallery as opposed to a museum? Is there empty space around individual paintings or are several placed in a group? Why did the curator do this? What is the parallel choice in theater? Why do so many galleries employ white space around the individual works of art? What information is placed on the cards under the paintings? What's the equivalent in the theater? What do you want your audience to know as background or context? How do curators create a path and journey through the show over time for a viewer? How do you enter and exit? What is the lighting like? What can you learn and use from these models?

ARCHITECTURE

Apply these *questions* to any combination of (1) the theater itself (auditorium, hall, outdoor vs. indoor, proscenium vs. arena vs. thrust); (2) the relationship between playing space and audience; (3) the piece itself; (4) the sets designed for the piece.

SIZE. How big or small is the *structure*? How much volume does it contain? How does the size of different buildings or rooms affect people differently? How can you use this in the theater?

MASS. How much mass is there vs. how much negative or empty space? What is the stage equivalent of doors and windows—the moments in the theater that allow us to enter or exit, to look outside, to let light in?

SHAPE. What shape does the architecture consist of? Is it angular or rounded? Are shapes in harmony or discord?

MATERIALS. What are the various materials that architects use? What are their different functional and expressive qualities? Is your Play-World full of wood, metal, glass, concrete?

AWARENESS OF LIGHT. How do architects consider lighting when designing their structures? What can you learn from this?

FLOW. How do different buildings allow flow from one space to another? How do plays do the same thing? How do you move inside of the architecture? Do small rooms open into larger ones, so that there is contraction and expansion? Are there hallways that make transitions gradual, or do you suddenly find yourself in a new space? How does this work for the characters in your piece? How does this work for your audience in the course of the evening? Does something meander, does it allow for choice on the part of the inhabitant, or does it tell you exactly where to go? How do solid objects contain flow?

TENSION AND COMPRESSION. Is the structure of the piece held together by compression or ex*tension*?

RHYTHM. How is rhythm used in architecture? Can you apply this to your work?

FILM

POINT OF VIEW. How does film use the camera's eye in different ways? How do you do this onstage? How does the audience look through a lens? Are you using a single point of view? Is it subjective or objective? How do you stage something completely from one character's subjective point of view? Is it how s/he sees things, feel things, remembers things?

SHOTS. What is, and how do you stage, an establishing shot, a tracking shot, a pan, a close-up, medium shot, long shot?

How do you see something from an extreme distance in theater? From overhead?

Note: The split screen is one of the few techniques that film has borrowed from live theater, and not vice versa. Theater quite organically provides a home for multiple and simultaneous imagery, leaving the point of focus up to the audience's discretion, whereas film typically limits the perspective to one point of view at any given moment.

EDITING. How do people edit film and how do you edit theater? How do you move from one moment or scene to another? Do you employ jump-cuts, cross-fades, dissolves? Can you superimpose? Are your units long or short?

SOUND TRACK. What do you hear when you listen to a movie sound track? How are films scored and why? What is ambient sound? Are there such things as aural close-ups? How do you create these in the theater? Are sounds *diegetic* or *non-diegetic*, i.e., can the characters hear the sounds, or only the audience? What moments require music? When does music get in the way or manipulate? What is voice-over and how can you use it in the theater?

TITLES AND SUBTITLES. Is there a credit sequence? Does it occur at the beginning or end of a film, and how does it affect you either way? How are opening credit sequences useful, and is there a device in the theater that serves the same purpose? Can we use the notion of subtitles (or title cards as they were used in silent film) in the theater?

GENRE. What qualities and devices belong to different genres? What makes up a genre? Do you want to embrace, comment on, or revolt against a given genre in your work? What specific film genres can we learn from and bring into the theater: spaghetti western, film noir, documentary, etc.?

DANCE

ABSTRACTION. How does form create content? How are stories organized and characters created in dance? How do choreographers think about time?

FORMS. What are different dance forms—polka, pas de deux, tango—and does each imply a different use of Shape, Tempo, intention? How can you use dance to work on a scene? How can two people onstage, even in a naturalistic play, engage in a minuet or a lindy or a slam dance?

ACCUMULATION. How does the reworking of thematic material affect the overall impact of the dance?

POETRY

RHYME. Is a poem rhymed or *un*rhymed? How would this translate into a theater piece?

RHYTHM. What is the meter? How does it scan?

FORM. Can you use the formal structure of a sonnet, quatrain or limerick to structure a theater piece? What does a haiku in the theater look like? Can a single line be a whole scene?

DEVICES. What literary devices do we find in poetry, and how can we transmute them into theatrical moments? What is *allusion* and *metaphor* and *simile*?

LITERATURE AND DRAMA

INSPIRATION. What makes a great novel? What makes a great play? What patterns emerge for you as an artist in what you love? What draws you in and moves you and stays with you? Why? How can you apply this to theater?

MOTIVATION. Is there intention, a character wanting something? Is there action? Is there obstacle? Is there conflict?

CHARACTER. What *is* character? Does someone change or stay the same? How active does the character's story have to be in order to engage you?

LANGUAGE. Do you respond to simple or complex language? Do you respond to words you know and say or words you don't know and have to look up? What pieces use a lot of words, and which only a few? Is there a kind of writing that turns you off? What's the equivalent of this in theater language or production approach?

THEME. What *is* theme? How directly or indirectly is it addressed in various works?

GENRE. What are various kinds of literature? Study the memoir, the roman à clef, the detective story, the exposé, the graphic novel, the epic, the short story, the melodrama, the cycle, the domestic drama, the musical. How does each work? What can you steal, incorporate, revise?

OTHER PLACES TO LOOK

We once asked a Composition group to list other art forms they could draw from, and the list included:

NEWSPAPER. Feature, hard news, editorials, etc.

FASHION. Foundations, layers, ornamentation, fabric, lines.

CIRCUS. The role of ringmaster, the three rings, feats, danger, humor.

OPERA. Aria, solo/duet/trio/quartet, the use of chorus, motifs.

MULTIMEDIA. Computers, video, electronic games and CD-ROMs, hyperlinks, navigation windows, cut-and-paste collages, windows, notions of interactive participation.

As well as everything from sculpture to comic books to magic to photography to calligraphy to cooking . . .

CHAPTER 17

VIEWPOINTS IN
UNEXPECTED PLACES

Viewpoints appears everywhere in life: in the way people move, the way animals flock, the way cars pass on the highway. Frequently, when someone first learns the names of the individual Viewpoints, they become obsessed with spotting them at work *everywhere*: "Did you see how those people over there responded *Kinesthetically* to each other?!" Of course, this is the way life always is and has been; but naming the Viewpoints allows us to dissect reality into something identifiable and perhaps repeatable onstage.

In this chapter we'll discuss some of the unexpected places where you can identify the Viewpoints at work in the theater and daily life, starting with playwriting and expanding outward to include diverse cultural staples, such as a baseball game and the cable television network Animal Planet.

VIEWPOINTS AND PLAYWRITING

In *writing* a text, Viewpoints and Composition can be used to generate material that the playwright can:

- Transcribe exactly
- Edit, using only some moments and not others
- Rewrite and shape
- Use as a jumping-off point or inspiration.

In *reading* a text we can find multiple examples of how the elements we've discussed in previous chapters are employed. For example, addressing three of the Viewpoints:

1. TEMPO. How quickly does a play move? What is the tempo of *The Lady from the Sea* as compared to *Glengarry Glen Ross*? How does Tempo express and differentiate character? Name some characters that speak or think slowly, and some that speed. Imagine playing a slow character at a fast tempo. Imagine a character whose internal tempo contrasts with her/his external one (i.e., s/he realizes things slowly, yet darts around the room).

2. DURATION. How long do things last in a given play? Are scenes short or long? Are they all of the same length or is there variety of duration (e.g., two short scenes followed by a long one followed by ten brief flashes)? Within each scene, are the events short or long? Is action drawn out or curtailed? How does the playwright use stage directions and create specificity of event with pause vs. beat vs. silence vs. a long silence? Does a character take a full page to tell her/his story or a single sentence? Is the play epic in length or a streamlined one-act? Why? What does your choice of duration say? The choices made give information, reveal character, build story and create meaning.

3. REPETITION. A playwright uses Repetition in language, in event, in character, in imagery and in structure. In the most basic form:

- Every time a character asks: "Do you love me? Do you?" the playwright is using Repetition. (Language)
- Every time a character attempts the same task, the playwright is using Repetition. (Event)
- Every time the same character enters, or every time two characters echo each other, the playwright is using Repetition. (Character)
- Every time the same eloquent object or symbol appears onstage, the playwright is using Repetition. (Imagery)
- Every time we return to a locale, the playwright is using Repetition. (Structure)

Additionally, a text can employ *internal* repetition (a character repeating herself/himself in language or action) or *external* repetition (a character, language, event repeating each other throughout the play).

Composition is the act of writing as a group, in time and space, using the language of the theater. Every director and performer and designer is a writer in the sense that we are all—*always*—creating meaning.

Additionally, whereas playwrights might tend to focus on creating meaning through the spoken word, they might also, in entering the universe of Viewpoints, begin to dream ways of writing images, impressions, sounds, movement.

VIEWPOINTS AND DIRECTING

Viewpoints provides a tool for the director to use with a company of actors in the rehearsal process; but it also provides a method of practice and implementation for her/him as well. A director can teach Viewpoints. A director can direct with Viewpoints. A director can practice Viewpoints in the way s/he talks to others and collaborates.

Viewpoints with Your Company

When determining how to use Viewpoints with actors in working on a project, consider the following:

1. Will I use Viewpoints to build ensemble?
2. Will I use Viewpoints as warm-up and training?
3. Will I use Viewpoints to generate material that I'll edit?
4. Will I use Viewpoints to stage scenes?

Viewpoints in Your Direction

When determining how to use Viewpoints in directing a production, consider:

1. How are each of the individual Viewpoints already present in the material? Which one(s) is most manifest? Do you imagine the same in the staging? How obvious will the use of Viewpoints be in your work, and why?

    How will you use Architecture, for instance? In opening up to the possibilities of Architecture, consider everything (from scratch) and as if for the first time: Where does theater happen? Where *can* theater happen? Does my piece belong in a traditional or nontraditional theater space? Study the space itself and determine how actively you will *use* it (not what is built inside of it). Consider all possibilities of how your audience might enter, sit or stand, be in relationship to the playing area(s). Take nothing for granted. Related to your use of Architecture are:

    □ TOPOGRAPHY. Is there a territory, a visible or invisible landscape, in your playing space, with defined areas, shapes, hills, valleys, etc.? Additionally, for both the entire production and also for every scene you stage, you will make choices about the size and shape of the playing space. Rather than assuming that every scene occurs in a general area, roughly "center-ish, kind of big enough" to hold the action; ask instead if a scene wants to live *in one space* or *on a grid* or *in a tiny sliver of space* all the way upstage against the back wall or *in a pool of light* downstage right. In making topographical choices, scene by scene, you create an unfolding meaning over time. The overall Topography of your production will be revealed to an audience over the course of the evening.

- TEMPO, DURATION, KINESTHETIC RESPONSE, REPETI-TION, SHAPE, GESTURE AND SPATIAL RELATIONSHIP. How do you visualize these Viewpoints in the work? Go through each individual Viewpoint in terms of the play itself. Go through each View-point in terms of the characters within the play.

2. Viewpoints is also critical in determining how a production moves, i.e., its transitions, set moves, light cues, sounds cues. Tempo, Duration, Kinesthetic Response and Repetition are all about your sense of timing. (See Viewpoints and Design, below.)

Viewpoints in Your Being

Teaching and practicing Viewpoints with your company helps you observe and articulate the individual Viewpoints around you. By sharing, you are practicing. Be sure to practice what you preach. If you say that being open is important, then be open. If you say that no one needs to feel the pressure to come up with stuff alone, then take that pressure off yourself. If you say it is important to use what you are given rather than what you want, then use what you are given.

Work hard in every day of rehearsal to exemplify the philo-sophic goals of Viewpoints:

- ☐ Listen
- ☐ Pay attention
- ☐ Be open
- ☐ Change
- ☐ Respond
- ☐ Surprise yourself
- ☐ Use accidents
- ☐ Work with fearlessness and abandon and an open heart.

VIEWPOINTS AND DESIGN

Designers too work with Viewpoints, whether or not they are aware of it or use the specific vocabulary. Designers can employ the principles of Viewpoints in the design studio alone, while dreaming or drafting, and also in the rehearsal studio, by allowing Viewpoints to bring them into a design world closer in proximity to the actors and the daily discoveries of rehearsal.

In applying the fundamentals of Viewpoints to design, a set designer will obviously consider the basics such as Architecture (mass, color, texture, volume, etc.), Topography, Shape, etc. But there is an extension of how one might think of the Viewpoints in application. Viewpoints implies a world where nothing is fixed and anything can happen. How does one design a stage space that encourages (rather than inhibits) this mutability? A space inspired by Viewpoints is one in which fixed place does not necessarily exist: place changes, transforms, returns, according to what happens inside of it. In this way, it is often helpful to think of the space as an *arena* rather than a *set*. Designing a space that cannot change or a space that cannot interact is anathema to Viewpoints.

Ask yourself: What *is* the space, the arena? Is it a dreamscape, the inside of someone's head, a ruin, a temple, a memory? Making these choices will tell you not only what the space looks and feels like but how it operates—the rules for movement and transition. In lighting design, we could easily go to a light plot and point out how Topography and Spatial Relationship and

Repetition exist in the plot itself. The same in costume sketches: the use of *color* and *texture* (Architecture of clothing), the use of Shape and Repetition, etc.

But what can Viewpoints teach us that is *new* to how we approach design work? Viewpoints invites designers into the rehearsal room, it gets designers working *with*, as opposed to alone. Open the process to include them. When working with Viewpoints in rehearsal you are constantly pressing to "use what you have." So often a company will discover amazing moments with a door, a dolly, a broom, a chair—is there no way to translate it into production? Usually, through a collective unconscious agreement between director/actor/designer, we bind ourselves by what has been predetermined (the design) and are not truly open to what actually occurs (the rehearsal). Get the designer into the room.

Similarly, get the actors onto the set, or get the set into the room, as early and as fully as possible. There is only one way to create theater in which the set functions as partner, where it is used and lived in and becomes expressive, and that is by including it early on. If reality absolutely prohibits this process, make sure that when you do "move onto the stage," you take time to allow the actors to Viewpoint in the space. Explore the architecture. Discover the acoustics. Otherwise, you will find yourself with yet another production where you could lift the entire set and replace it with another, and few would register the difference. Embrace the notion that a set is not background—it is space, it is an *arena*, it is a context within which things occur, and it is there to *help* those things occur.

If you are able to have the designer(s) in rehearsal for even a short amount of time, do Open Viewpoints with a theme related to the show. Create specific Compositions that the designer(s) can watch and discuss with the group. Ask the company to make a piece on how light functions in your Play-World. What are the sources of light? Are all characters lit equally? Do some belong more to shadow than light? How is light a character itself in your piece? Ask each company member to bring in an article of clothing that expresses their character and to make a portrait Composition, which includes how they use this article, why they love it, where they found it, etc. And, above all, make sure that your designer(s) understand that the work is not meant to dictate but to inspire. If a designer can leave the room with one new seed of inspiration, it was time well spent.

In tech-ing a show, Viewpoints of Time is present in every decision about cues and transitions. Not only are we paying primary attention to Tempo (How fast does a unit travel onstage?) and Duration (How long does it take to complete?), but we must also recognize that the most powerful choices we make about whether or not transitions are effective have to do with Kinesthetic Response. In determining how a light cue slowly fades then bumps out just as the music comes on, which continues until the set is in place, which finishes just as the music ends and the lights bump back on, you are dealing fundamentally with the *Kinesthetic Response among movement, light and sound.*

Light and sound can respond Kinesthetically not only to each other but to movement outside themselves. A set piece moves, but so do the gestures and text of an actor. Imagine moments in which light responds Kinesthetically to a gesture made by an actor, *and*, vice versa, imagine an actor responding Kinesthetically to light flickering or growing unbearably bright. In performance, Viewpoints finds expression not only actor-to-actor, but in actor-to-light-to-sound and back again. Everyone from the performer to the stage manager to the technicians is engaged in a giant collective game of Viewpoints.

And finally, too, we must recognize and embrace the fact that the game not only involves the audience, but elects them as *the* scene partner with whom we are all, ultimately, playing.

VIEWPOINTS EVERYWHERE: IN SPORTS, WAITING TABLES AND THE ANIMAL KINGDOM

On June 17, 2000, an article appeared in the *New York Times* on then New York Yankee baseball player Chuck Knoblauch. The article, by Erica Goode, began:

A desperately frustrated Yankee second baseman and a nineteenth century Russian novelist have little in common, one might think.

But, in a way, Chuck Knoblauch is in the same pickle as Leo Tolstoy was as a child, when his brother challenged him to stand in a corner until he could stop thinking about white bears. Tolstoy, the legend has it, stood in that corner for quite a while, with white bears trooping through his mind. Tolstoy's brush with obsession was trivial, but Knoblauch, who left a ball game in frustration Thursday night after his inability to make simple throws to first base resulted in three errors, has a lot more at stake . . .

The problem, sports psychologists surmised yesterday, is that an action that Knoblauch has instinctually performed thousands of times is suddenly the object of conscious thought.

And in a related article by James C. McKinley, Jr.:

[One lifelong Yankee fan] said: "You can see he's thinking too much. He's not reacting." . . . Others said the cure was both simple and complicated. Knoblauch, they said, needs to empty his mind and just play. [For as] Yogi Berra once said when he was a rookie, "I can't think and hit at the same time."

From sports to Zen Buddhism to *The Wizard of Oz*, the refrain is echoed time and again:

"Thinking is stinking," says the baseball axiom.

_____ says the Zen master.

"Pay no attention to the man behind the curtain," says the Wizard.

When Knoblauch later described the instant of thought that prohibited him from throwing to first base, he might as well have been discussing Viewpoints as baseball. He said:

"The goal is to react spontaneously."

There is a phrase in sports, "In the Zone," which provides a useful analogue for the state of openness and flow one hopes to achieve in Viewpoints training. Legendary baseball hitter Ted Williams commented that, in this state, sometimes he could see the seams on a pitched baseball. Gymnast Carol Johnston found that on some days she experienced the balance beam as wider, so "any worry of falling off disappeared."

Further exploration of the *In the Zone* phenomenon suggests that common characteristics include:

- RELAXATION. No extremes. Attainment without consciousness of striving. The mind calm; the body tuned, fed and watered; peace within the physical self; peace within the spirit. Strength, ease, readiness without fear.
- CONFIDENCE. Belief in yourself, in your fellow athletes, in the integrity of the sport. Pride in the hard work of training, in the history of the competition, stretching back through the centuries. Victory in the mind, long before the moment when the spectators' first roar washes through the stadium.
- FOCUS. Complete absorption, total, absolute, without reservation. The past is without form, the future without failure. The task, the need, the now is all that you can know.
- EFFORTLESSNESS. Ebb and flow in the grasp of something greater than human frailty, smooth and inexorable, beyond the inconveniences of gravity, fatigue, failure. Graceful, easy, connected and light.
- SELF-CONTAINMENT. Internal harmony, thoughts and emotions, senses external and internal, heart and muscle and mind blending together in the automaticity that dedicated

practice brings. No discord; no hesitation; no dissonance between the decision and the action; instinct replaced by something higher, yet something more basic than reason; a strength of being that takes the human being to a level so far beyond day-to-day awkwardness that every movement becomes poetry.

☐ JOY. Pure and innocent delight, childlike happiness in the velvet flow of achievement, fulfillment won at hard cost, with even the sting of pain and the ache of exhaustion warming and kindling the pleasure of attainment, the love of the sport for all that it has been and all that it will be.

The parallels between this philosophy of sports and that of Viewpoints are both astonishing and, once realized, very obvious. Both sports and Viewpoints involve *play*, the kind of play young children engage in—that of reacting to something that happens in a spontaneous fashion, without self-consciousness, judgment or hesitation. In sports, as in so many other things in life, we can once again witness the lessons of Viewpoints in action. We continue to learn about the timeless art of taking what is given you (whether a ground ball, a toy figure or a sudden move onstage) and out of it, making something wonderful.

There are as many ways to describe this state, these actions, as there are cultures and activities. There is "the Oceanic state," coined by Sigmund Freud; there is the concept of "Flow" in Mihaly Csikszentmihalyi's *Flow: The Psychology of Optimal Experience* (Harper Perennial, New York, 1991); the "Peak-Experiences" defined by A. H. Maslow in "Religious Aspects of Peak-Experiences" (in his book *Religions, Values, and Peak-Experiences*, Penguin, New York, 1994); and essayist Diane Ackerman's phrase "Deep Play," which she borrowed from eighteenth century philosopher Jeremy Bentham for describing those moments when "levered by ecstasy, one springs out of one's mind."

We once asked a group of students where else in life they recognized Viewpoints at work. The answers flew. One young woman talked about her waitressing job and how she suddenly became aware of how she and her co-workers were Viewpointing:

"It's a dance," she said, "one person will be up at the register while another leans below to grab a ketchup bottle from a shelf, and without ever looking at each other we know exactly where the other is and what they're doing. If we lost that awareness, accidents would start happening—you know, plates flying, drinks spilling." She went on to describe the difficulty of maneuvering with a tray of mixed drinks through the bar crowd on a busy night: "The only way I can do it is with *soft focus*—I've been doing that forever, I just never had a name for it."

Another student talked about his new favorite television station: Animal Planet. Since starting Viewpoints training, he had gone home every night to obsessively watch, in his exact words, "Flamingos and rhinoceri and beetles doing the Viewpoints."

Watch the way animals flock. Watch the way a school of fish shifts direction as if one. Watch people waiting for a bus or train—when one person leans out to check for the oncoming vehicle, others immediately follow. Watch people on the subway or watching a movie—when one person shifts weight or angle, there is a ripple reaction that follows from one to another.

The ultimate lesson of Viewpoints, after all, might be one of humility. We did not invent a system that the world mirrors. Rather, it is the natural world itself that holds such timeless and consistent patterns of behavior. It is our struggle to name the patterns and then apply them to our art.

AFTERWORD

Working with SITI Company

ANNE BOGART

In 1992, with the help of Japanese director Tadashi Suzuki, I founded SITI Company, which quickly became the core of my creative existence. Early on in the life of SITI, it became clear that training constitutes the basic agreement of the ensemble—the glue that keeps us *questioning* and evolving. Viewpoints and Suzuki's method of actor training are the foundation of our physical and vocal training. Composition work forms our approach to rehearsal, whether in the creation of original work or classical plays, new plays, dance-theater or opera. This ongoing training and study quickly sharpened SITI into an efficient and prolific group of artists.

Based in New York City, SITI Company is comprised of twenty-one strong-willed individuals: ten actors, four designers, one playwright and a production team. The company's mission is threefold: (1) to create, perform and tour new productions; (2) to provide ongoing training for young theater artists; and (3) to foster opportunities for cultural exchange with theater professionals and audiences around the globe.

The company is on tour and in performance for long periods every year. We also spend a lot of time running workshops and training programs around the world. And we spend lots of time in rehearsal. But, *always*, we find time to train together.

We begin every rehearsal with about forty minutes of training—twenty minutes of Suzuki training (see Bibliography) and then a fifteen-minute Viewpoints session with music, followed by a *very* brief critique. Before every performance, except during technical rehearsal days, the company trains together. When not working on a particular production, we find ways to continue our training practice together.

All of the actors in the company are also excellent teachers. When not in performance, company members can usually be found teaching. We offer training programs in New York City, Los Angeles, Ohio, Kentucky and Ireland. Every June in Saratoga Springs, New York, sixty-five theater professionals from around the world join us for four remarkably intensive weeks of training.

Composition is also a tool that we use as well as teach. The time set aside for Composition work allows us to sketch ideas that we can show to one another. This activity keeps the rehearsals from getting too heady or academic. We believe in the Brechtian "show me" approach to generating stage moments. Rather than talking too much, we insist on sketching ideas onstage immediately.

Viewpoints and Composition serve as shorthand during the heat of a rehearsal. Sharing a common vocabulary streamlines the process: "Your Spatial Relationship is weak in that moment, can you fix it?" or "I think that the scene needs more acceleration." When we are stuck, sometimes we Viewpoint a scene until we find the hidden key. The Compositions that we create induce an instant history—a reservoir of references and ideas to draw from. These approaches work for us in a very practical sense. But the approaches are not a "technique" and they are certainly not dogma. They are an evolving practice of investigation into the language of the theater and penetration into the mysteries of a play.

When I first came into contact with Composition and Viewpoints, through the profound influence of Aileen Passloff and Mary Overlie, I felt instantly that "something is right in the world." At the time I could not put these feelings into words, but I could pursue my excitement by trying out these ideas myself in my work with other people. So I did. And this pursuit brought consistent insight and a rehearsal atmosphere where the creative act was shared. This sharing was galvanizing and necessary and far preferable to any other way of working. This approach is, for me, more than a technique, more than a way of keeping a company together; it is a philosophy of being in the world that I can believe in. Inside this philosophy we don't have answers; rather, we express our points of view about things: *our Viewpoints.* These processes provide windows through which one might, for a short time, see more clearly.

Each SITI Company member has contributed to the evolution of Viewpoints and Composition. Barney O'Hanlon is perhaps the most adventurous practitioner and teacher of Viewpoints. Before joining SITI Company, he studied both with Mary Overlie and me, and he has become a radical innovator. Leon Ingulsrud and J. Ed Araiza are both directors as well as actors in SITI and have used Composition work extensively and with remarkable results. They both keep me on my toes. Sound Designer Darron West brought music and sound to Viewpoints, and I have to run at top speed to keep up with him. Actors: Ellen Lauren, Stephen Webber, Kelly Maurer, Will Bond, Akiko Aizawa, Susan Hightower and Tom Nelis. Designers: Neil Patel, James Schuette, Mimi Jordan Sherin and Brian Scott. Playwrights: Chuck Mee and Jocelyn Clarke. Managers: Megan Wanlass Szalla and Elizabeth Moreau. These are the people who inspire innovation, flexibility, joy and growth. SITI Company keeps me honest.

As I move from one season to the next with members of SITI Company, I am indebted to the influences that led me to them, and I am grateful to the Company for their patience, interest, sweat and humor.

Working with the Steppenwolf Ensemble, or An Old Dog Learning New Tricks

TINA LANDAU

I had more of an impression of what Steppenwolf was than a first-hand knowledge. I had only seen two of their productions and had only been to Chicago twice (briefly) in my life. When I thought of Steppenwolf, I thought kitchen sinks, dirty walls, and people screaming, throwing chairs, breaking furniture, loving, sweating, wrestling and generally living life out onstage at a high pitch. And this wasn't wholly unappealing to me. But I came from a different world. When I thought Steppenwolf, I thought "method acting" and "naturalism," notions less unappealing than frightening. Music and history and poetry—those I could deal with; hand props and living rooms and behavior—I was less sure about. How would I fit in? Could I communicate with the actors and vice versa? Would they think I was a martian?

But a distant voice also told me, "Steppenwolf: abandon, spontaneity, muscle, extremity, danger . . ." And I hoped somewhere that we would find common ground. And so, in 1996, the person some of them thought of as "the New York City avant-garde director-type" packed her bags and took off to direct at Steppenwolf. I went with trepidation and skepticism, plagued by images of, well, oil and water.

Frank Galati, a Steppenwolf ensemble member, had seen my production of *Floyd Collins* (which I wrote with Adam Guettel) at Playwrights Horizons in New York. He had gone back to Chicago and told Martha Lavey, Steppenwolf's Artistic Director, that she should see the show and bring it to Chicago. She came, liked the work, and in the course of our discussions we determined together that it wasn't the right time or place for *Floyd* (Steppenwolf had never produced a full-blown musical, the costs were prohibitive, etc.). But Martha invited me to direct something else and we settled on a new Chuck Mee play, *Time to Burn*, based on Gorky's *The Lower Depths*. It was material that seemed to bridge our worlds:

theatrical, as only Chuck can write, but also fluid and lyrical and human, real people in real time in a real place and, above all, an ensemble piece.

Just before I left for Chicago, I was speaking to someone about Viewpoints and they said, "Well, you know the famous Steppenwolf story, don't you?" "No," I said. Uh-oh, I thought. "Well, a young director was working with the ensemble on a new play and gave them an exercise relating to gesture, and there they were working, when suddenly one of the Steppenwolf ensemble members threw down her notebook and started screaming, 'We don't do gesture work here! We don't do gesture work ANYWHERE! In fact, we don't DO gesture work! In fact, I don't DO gestures!!!'"

When I introduced Viewpoints on my first day of rehearsal, I joked about this story. I asked the company simply to acknowledge whatever preconceptions and skepticism they had, and to open to the work nonetheless. I asked them to work with an open heart toward me, toward the process, toward each other, toward themselves. To play like kids just for this one day. They didn't have to like it or understand its use, but just *do* it.

The next day we were talking as a group when Mike Nussbaum raised his hand and said, "I'd like to make a statement to everyone." Now Mike is a stalwart of Chicago theater, a legend to many, by far the senior royalty in the cast (from his age, his talent and his experience). My "uh-oh" returned. But then Mike said, "I have only one thing to contribute and for the first time I really know what it means: you *can* teach an old dog new tricks."

The following season I wrote and directed *Space* (after which I was invited to join the ensemble), featuring ensemble members Mariann Mayberry, Robert Breuler, Amy Morton and Tom Irwin. On the first day of Viewpoints, Mariann soared. Bob kept smashing an orange into his forehead out of some need to deflect and entertain us all, Tom rolled his eyes a lot and Amy, in a brave attempt to bust through her discomfort and fear, kept looking at walls, taking aim like a bull, and then running at them to throw herself into the plaster, full throttle. On the second day, all four of them soared. And, on the third day, they told me who the ensemble member was who had proclaimed: "I don't *do* gestures."

I had the joy of working with her for the first time in my production of *The Ballad of Little Jo*, Steppenwolf's first musical. Her name is Rondi Reed (some ensemble folk call her "Dame Reed"). Rondi blew into rehearsal on the first day and bellowed: "Okay, so what is all this Viewpoints bullshit?!" She laughed, as did I, but four hours later Rondi not only *did* Gestures, but Shape, Architecture, Topography, etc. Over a beer one night she confessed that the previous director "didn't even know what a gesture was *herself*, let alone how to talk to actors about them! Of course I do gestures—we all do, every day, onstage and off—but not when it *takes away from* rather than *adds to* my life onstage. This director didn't love actors or acting; she loved her own ideas." (I contend that there is no such thing as a *diva*; only great artists working with people who are more lazy, or great and scared artists looking for their net.)

The strands of this story have a happy ending, for the time being: the Steppenwolf ensemble is interested in Viewpoints. Some are merely interested enough to ask: "What *is* that, anyway?" Others have started showing up at my classes at the Steppenwolf Summer School, and one is even applying to the four-week SITI intensive in Saratoga next spring. Oil and water. Hmmm.

The influence works both ways of course. Through these extraordinary artists, I have been inspired and challenged once again to deeply reflect on the art of acting. How do you direct actors? What kind of language constitutes useful direction? How do great actors (like these at Steppenwolf) think and play and work? What makes their acting so great? What do I value in acting? And if the answer is depth, vulnerability, rawness, surprise, spontaneity, soul, danger and, above all, *truth*, how can I fuel these with Viewpoints?

Yes, Viewpoints can be used to make incredibly sophisticated and intricate pieces of choreography. Eloquent form, let's say. But personally, Viewpoints continues to interest me more as a way *toward* emotion than *away* from it (which isn't to say form can't create emotion; of course it can, and that is one of the fundamentals of this book). I'm interested in the *increased* power a

Steppenwolf actor has onstage when s/he is working from both the psychology of motivation and intention *and* the physicality of Kinesthetic Response and Tempo, for instance. I believe not in the superiority of one process over the other but in *both*, together, fighting, alternating, informing. Inner psychology *and* outer form. Research the piece *and* dream it. Learn as much as you can *and* let it go. Prepare *and* then forget. Use everything available to you to be in the present moment.

You see, I've discovered the Steppenwolf approach and the Viewpoints approach are not so very different after all. My misconception was based on surface appearances, styles of work. In both cases, the imperatives are identical:

□ Listen
□ Work off your partner
□ Let go, and trust
□ Be in the moment
□ Be in your body
□ Use your body
□ Surprise each other
□ *Do*, rather than *feel*
□ Work with danger
□ Work with unpredictability
□ Work in the extremes
□ Commit your entire being
□ Work from your passion
□ Care for your audience and tell a story
□ Play as *one*
□ Be an ensemble.

There's another thing I've learned from Steppenwolf. It's not: "Yes *and* . . ." or "The same only different," but it too possesses a quirky and self-explanatory name. We call it: "I cry bullshit." I learned this from the likes of Tom and Amy, Laurie Metcalf, Gary Sinise, Terry Kinney and Jeff Perry. It's a favor the ensemble does for each other, and they've developed this technique over twenty-five years together in basements, churches, and now in their three performance spaces on North Halsted Street in

Chicago. If you're watching rehearsal and something happens onstage that is false, contrived, not believable (it could be a move, an acting choice, a line), you are encouraged (not required) by Steppenwolf Law to raise your hand as you would in class and call out: "I cry bullshit!" This, to me, is where Steppenwolf and Viewpoints most gloriously meet—in their commitment to ensemble. We are what we are because of each other. I am open to you, for I trust you will help me become all I can, in my life, in my art, and onstage.

BIBLIOGRAPHY

The following list represents sources—from many disciplines and through many years—which have inspired us. Some of these works are mentioned specifically in our book, and all the others could have been. This list is profoundly subjective and varied—a conglomeration of the books, art, and deep thinking that have most influenced our work in Viewpoints and Composition.

RUDOLF ARNHEIM
Visual Thinking
University of California Press, Berkeley, 1969

GASTON BACHELARD
The Poetics of Space: The Classic Look at How We Experience Intimate Places
Beacon Press, Boston, 1994

SALLY BANES
Democracy's Body: Judson Dance Theater, 1962–1964
Duke University Press, Durham, NC, 1993

Terpsichore in Sneakers: Post-Modern Dance
Wesleyan University Press, Middletown, CT, 1987

EUGENIO BARBA; translated by Richard Fowler
The Paper Canoe: A Guide to Theatre Anthropology
Routledge, New York, 1995

EUGENIO BARBA and NICOLA SAVARESE; translated by Richard
Fowler; edited and compiled by Richard Gough
A Dictionary of Theatre Anthropology: The Secret Art of the Performer
Centre for Performance Research, Routledge, New York, 1991

ANN MARIE SEWARD BARRY
Visual Intelligence: Perception, Image, and Manipulation in Visual
Communication
State University of New York Press, Albany, 1997

JEAN BAUDRILLARD; translated by Sheila Faria Glaser
Simulacra and Simulation (The Body, in Theory: Histories of Cultural
Materialism)
University of Michigan Press, Ann Arbor, 1995

PETER BROOK
The Empty Space (A Book about the Theatre: Deadly, Holy, Rough, Immediate)
Touchstone, New York, 1996

ITALO CALVINO
Six Memos for the Next Millennium
Harvard University Press, Cambridge, MA, 1988

JOSEPH CAMPBELL
The Hero with a Thousand Faces
Princeton University Press, Princeton, 1973

ELIAS CANETTI; translated by Victor Gollancz Ltd.
Crowds and Power
Farrar, Straus and Giroux, New York, 1984

JOSEPH CHAIKEN
The Presence of the Actor
Theatre Communications Group, New York, 1991

MICHAEL CHEKHOV; edited by Mel Gordon
On the Technique of Acting: The First Complete Edition of Chekhov's
Classic To the Actor
HarperCollins, New York, 1991

HAROLD CLURMAN; Introduction by **STELLA ADLER**
The Fervent Years: The Group Theatre & the '30s
Da Capo Press, Inc., New York, 1983

ANDREW COOPER
Playing in the Zone: Exploring the Spiritual Dimensions of Sports
Shambhala Publications, Boston, 1998

MIHALY CSIKSZENTMIHALYI
Creativity: Flow and the Psychology of Discovery and Invention
Harper Perennial, New York, 1997

Finding Flow: The Psychology of Engagement with Everyday Life
Basic Books, New York, 1998

Flow: The Psychology of Optimal Experience
Harper Perennial, New York, 1991

EDWARD DE BONO
Lateral Thinking: Creativity Step by Step
Harper Perennial, New York, 1990

AGNES DE MILLE
Martha: The Life and Work of Martha Graham
Random House, New York, 1991

DECLAN DONNELLEN
The Actor and the Target
Theatre Communications Group, New York, 2002

GRETEL EHRLICH
The Solace of Open Spaces
Penguin Books, New York, 1986

T. S. ELIOT
Four Quartets
A Harvest Book, Harcourt, Inc., Orlando, 1968

PHILIP FISHER
The Vehement Passions
Princeton University Press, Princeton, 2003

SIMONE FORTI
Handbook in Motion
The Press of the Nova Scotia College of Art and Design, Halifax, 1974

MALCOLM GLADWELL
Blink: The Power of Thinking without Thinking
Little, Brown and Company, New York, 2005

ERVING GOFFMAN
Behavior in Public Places: Notes on the Social Organization of Gatherings
Greenwood Press, Westport, CT, 1980

Frame Analysis: An Essay on the Organization of Experience
Northeastern University Press, Lebanon, NH, 1986

The Presentation of Self in Everyday Life
An Anchor Book, Bantam Doubleday Dell Publishing Group, Inc.,
New York, 1959

JERZY GROTOWSKI; edited by EUGENIO BARBA; introduction by
PETER BROOK
Towards a Poor Theatre
Routledge, New York, 2002

CHARLES HAMPDEN-TURNER
Maps of the Mind
Scribner, Simon & Schuster, New York, 1981

RICHARD HORNBY
The End of Acting: A Radical View
Applause Books, New York, 1995

SUSAN A. JACKSON and MIHALY CSIKSZENTMIHALYI
Flow in Sports
Human Kinetics Publishers, Champaign, IL, 1999

JULIAN JAYNES
The Origin of Consciousness in the Breakdown of the Bicameral Mind
Mariner Books, Houghton Mifflin Company, New York, 2000

ROBERT EDMOND JONES and DELBERT UNRUH
Towards a New Theatre: The Lectures of Robert Edmond Jones
Limelight Editions, Pompton Plains, NJ, 1992

TADEUSZ KANTOR; translated and edited by Michal Kobialka
A Journey Through Other Spaces: Essays and Manifestos, 1944–1990
University of California Press, Berkeley, 1993

SØREN KIERKEGAARD; translated and edited by Howard V. Hong
and Edna H. Hong
Fear and Trembling/Repetition: Kierkegaard's Writings, Volume 6
Princeton University Press, Princeton, 1983

GUNTHER R. KRESS and THEO VAN LEEUWEN
Reading Images: The Grammar of Visual Design
Routledge, New York, 1996

MADELEINE L'ENGLE
A Wrinkle in Time
Bantam Doubleday Dell Books for Young Readers, New York, 1962

JERRY MANDER
Four Arguments for the Elimination of Television
Harper Perennial, New York, 2002

A. H. MASLOW
Religions, Values, and Peak-Experiences
Penguin, New York, 1994

The plays of CHARLES L. MEE, JR., are available at "the (re)making
project" website at: http://charlesmee.org/html/plays.html

SANFORD MEISNER and DENNIS LONGWELL
Sanford Meisner on Acting
Vintage, Random House, New York, 1987

DAN MILLMAN
Body Mind Mastery: Creating Success in Sport and Life
New World Library, Novato, CA, 1999

STEPEN NACHMANOVITCH
Free Play: Improvisation in Life and Art
Jeremy P. Tarcher, Penguin Putnam Inc., New York, 1990

YVONNE RAINER
A Woman Who . . . : Essays, Interviews, Scripts
PAJ Books: Art + Performance, The Johns Hopkins University Press,
Baltimore, 1999

YVONNE RAINER and SID SACHS
Yvonne Rainer: Radical Juxtapositions 1961–2002
University of the Arts, Philadelphia (distributed by Distributed Art
Publishers, Inc., New York), 2003

JOHN J. RATEY, M.D.
*A User's Guide to the Brain: Perception, Attention, and the Four Theaters
of the Brain*
Vintage, Random House, New York, 2002

THOMAS RICHARDS and JERZY GROTOWSKI
At Work with Grotowski on Physical Actions
Routledge, New York, 1996

RICHARD SENNETT
The Fall of Public Man
W. W. Norton & Company, New York, 1992

TADASHI SUZUKI; translated by Thomas Rimer
The Way of Acting: The Theatre Writings of Tadashi Suzuki
Theatre Communications Group, New York, 1986

ANDREY TARKOVSKY; translated by Kitty Hunter-Blair
Sculpting in Time: Reflections on the Cinema
University of Texas Press, Austin, 1989

HENDEL TEICHER, editor
Trisha Brown: Dance and Art in Dialogue, 1961–2001
The MIT Press, Cambridge, MA, 2002

FRANÇOIS TRUFFAUT
Hitchcock/Truffaut
A Touchstone Book, Simon & Schuster, New York, 1985

JEANETTE WINTERSON
Art Objects: Essays on Ecstasy and Effrontery
Vintage, Random House, New York, 1997

ZEAMI; translated by J. Thomas Rimer; edited by Masakazu Yamazaki
On the Art of the No Drama: The Major Treatises of Zeami
Princeton University Press, Princeton, 1984

ANNE BOGART is Artistic Director of SITI Company, which she founded with Japanese director Tadashi Suzuki in 1992. She is a recipient of two OBIE awards, a Bessie Award and a Guggenheim Fellowship. She is a professor at Columbia University, where she runs the Graduate Directing Program. Recent works with SITI include *Intimations for Saxophone* by Sophie Treadwell; Shakespeare's *A Midsummer Night's Dream*; *Death and the Ploughman* by Michael West; *La Dispute* by Marivaux; *Short Stories*; *Score* by Jocelyn Clarke; *bobrauschenbergamerica* by Charles L. Mee, Jr.; *Room* by Jocelyn Clarke; *War of the Worlds* by Naomi Iizuka; *Cabin Pressure*; *The Radio Play*; *Alice's Adventures*; *Culture of Desire*; *Bob* by Jocelyn Clarke; *Going, Going, Gone*; *Small Lives/Big Dreams*; *The Medium*; Noël Coward's *Hay Fever* and *Private Lives*; August Strindberg's *Miss Julie*; and Charles L. Mee, Jr.'s *Orestes*. She is the author of *A Director Prepares* published by Routledge Press, New York, 2001.

TINA LANDAU is a freelance writer, director and teacher, as well as member of the Steppenwolf Theatre Company in Chicago. She is a graduate of Yale College and A.R.T.'s Institute for Advanced Theatre Training at Harvard, having returned to teach at both, as well as at New York University, Columbia University, Saratoga International Theater Institute (SITI), University of Chicago, Northwestern and UCSD. She is a former TCG/NEA Director Fellow, an NEA Artistic Associate and has received major grants from the Rockefeller, Princess Grace, W. Alton Jones, and Pew foundations. Original work that Tina both wrote and directed includes *Theatrical Essays* (Steppenwolf), *Beauty* (La Jolla Playhouse), *Space* (Steppenwolf; The Public Theater, New York; Center Theatre Group/Mark Taper Forum, Los Angeles), *Floyd*

Collins (Playwrights Horizons, New York; Old Globe, San Diego; Goodman, Chicago), *Dream True* (Vineyard Theatre, New York), *Stonewall* (En Garde Arts, New York) and *1969* (Actors Theatre of Louisville). At Steppenwolf, Tina has directed *Cherry Orchard*, *The Time of Your Life* (also at Seattle Repertory Theatre; A.C.T., San Francisco), *Maria Arndt*, *The Ballad of Little Jo*, *Berlin Circle* and *And Time to Burn*. In New York, her work includes the Broadway revival of *Bells Are Ringing*, *Miracle Brothers* (Vineyard Theatre), *Myths and Hymns* (The Public Theater), *Orestes* and *Trojan Women* (En Garde Arts), as well as *Of Thee I Sing* (Papermill Playhouse, Millburn, NJ) and *A Midsummer Night's Dream* (McCarter Theatre Center, Princeton; Papermill Playhouse).